MARVEL

BIG BOOK OF FUN

Parragon

Bath • New York • Cologne • Melbourne • Delhi
Hong Kong • Shenzhen • Singapore • Amsterdam

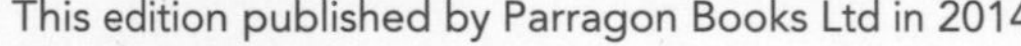

This edition published by Parragon Books Ltd in 2014

Parragon Books Ltd
Chartist House
15–17 Trim Street
Bath BA1 1HA, UK
www.parragon.com

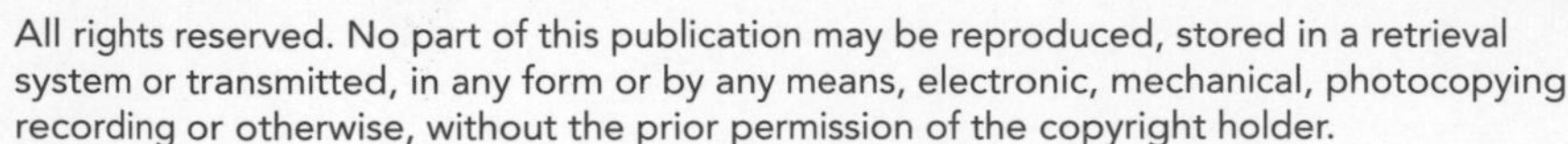

ISBN 978-1-4723-5627-7

Printed in China

MARVEL

MARVEL

the AMAZING SPIDER-MAN™

AN ORIGIN STORY

Peter enjoyed all his classes, but science was his favourite. He was the best student Midtown High had seen in many years and his teachers were very proud of him.

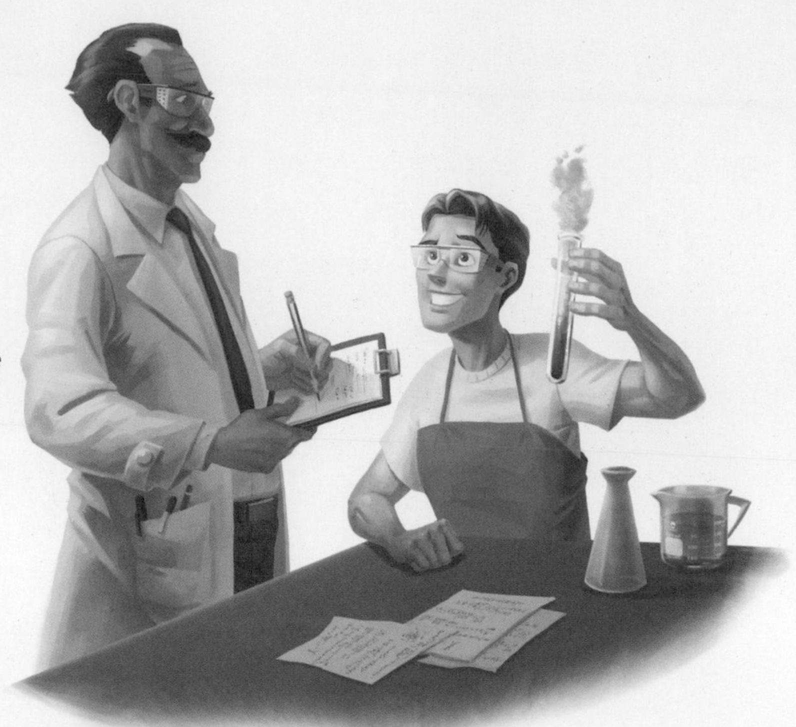

The only thing Peter loved more than science was his family. He lived with his Aunt May and his Uncle Ben in Queens, New York. And whenever Peter felt sad at school, he remembered he'd be home soon and he'd start to smile.

Even though some of the kids at school didn't like him, Peter never stopped trying to be friendly. He had heard about a great demonstration at the Science Hall. He asked the other kids if they wanted to join him.

The other students just laughed at Peter. One of them, a bully named Flash Thompson, even pushed him to the ground.

By the time Peter arrived at the Science Hall, he had forgotten all about his classmates' cruel actions. All he could think about was the experiment. He couldn't wait to see how the scientists would control a radioactive wave!

The rays were ready. Peter eagerly looked on. But so did something else. The demonstration was about to begin!

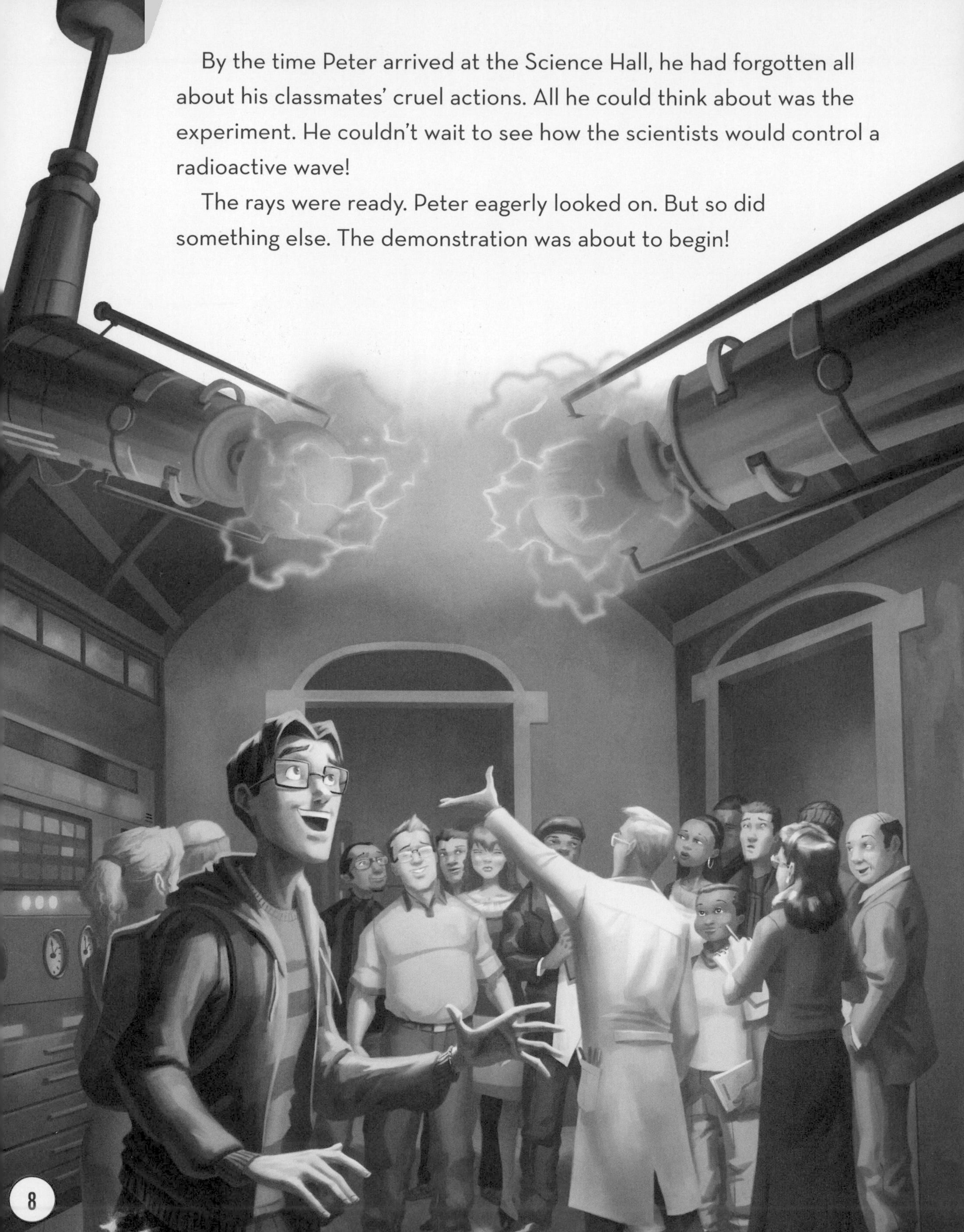

Peter was awed by the experiment. He was thrilled to be there in the company of such brilliant scientists. He wanted to be just like them – smart, talented ... amazing!

Everyone was so fascinated that no one noticed when something unplanned occurred. A spider descended between the rays just as they were activated. And as the radioactive spider fell, dying, it bit the nearest living thing. Which happened to be Peter Parker.

As soon as he was bitten, Peter felt weak and tired. The room began to spin. The scientists noticed that Peter looked ill and they offered to help him.

But Peter just wanted to get out of the dark laboratory and into the fresh air.

Peter felt a sudden, peculiar tingling in his head. It was an itching, urging, nagging feeling. The only thing he understood about it was that he was meant to react.

To do something.

So he did.

Peter was sure he was dreaming.

He couldn't really be climbing up a wall. Nobody could do that.

When he reached the roof, he grabbed on to a chimney – and crushed it! He didn't have that kind of strength.

Peter felt the tingly feeling again. This time it gave him the urge to spring. And so he jumped from one tall roof to another.

And when he wanted to go back down to the street, the same strange feeling told him the easiest way to get there was to climb down a clothesline.

Then, Peter realized he had started feeling different right after being bitten by that spider in the lab. Somehow the experiment must have affected the dying creature. And when it bit Peter, it transferred its power to him!

As he wandered home, amazed and half-dazed, a sign outside an old wrestling theatre caught his eye. It would be the perfect way to test all his newfound abilities.

Peter was ready to test his new powers on a brutish wrestler called Crusher Hogan. Peter wore a disguise so that no one would make fun of him if his plan didn't work.

He'd been teased and taunted enough. When Peter challenged him, Crusher Hogan laughed.

But Crusher soon found that he was very wrong to do so.

Peter was paid well for the victory. A man in the crowd even asked him if he'd want to be on TV. Things finally seemed to be going right for Peter.

Plus, Peter had his Aunt May and Uncle Ben at home. They were still doing everything they could to make him happy. His uncle had even saved up for a special microscope that Peter had wanted.

With his new microscope, Peter's experiments would be better than ever. Uncle Ben reminded him that knowledge and science were power. "And," Uncle Ben told Peter, "with great power comes great responsibility."

Peter was too excited to settle down. He used his new microscope, his chemistry set and his knowledge of science to create a very special fluid.

It had the strength and stickiness of a spider's silk. Then he created devices that could spin the fluid into a web the same way a spider would. He called them his web-shooters.

Finally, he designed a sleek new costume. Now all he needed was a stage name. He arrived at one as good as any other....

SPIDER-MAN!

Peter's TV appearances were a huge hit.

After all, who wouldn't be amazed by a Spider-Man climbing up walls and swinging from his own webs?

Soon everyone wanted a piece of Spider-Man. Peter was starting to feel important, wanted ... and powerful.

No one would ever be able to push him around again. Not when he had powers like these.

Peter got lost thinking about how wonderful his new life would be. He daydreamed about fame and celebrity. And when a security guard called for help down the studio hall, Peter ignored him.

The crook that the guard was chasing raced into a lift.

The doors closed and the thief escaped.

But Peter didn't care. He had great power. And from now on, he only needed to look out for one person – himself.

It didn't take long for Peter to forget about the guard and the escaped criminal. In fact, by the time he got home they were the furthest things from his mind. He was just happy to be with the people who loved him.

And in his spare time, when he was not studying or home with his family, Peter went out as the famous, spectacular Spider-Man!

But one night on his way home from a TV performance, Peter arrived to find something worrisome.

Peter knew something was terribly wrong and he was right. His Uncle Ben had been killed by a criminal. The police officers told Peter not to worry. They had the crook cornered at an old waterfront house.

Peter ran upstairs, put on his costume ...

and swooped over the city to avenge his uncle.
Peter was quicker and more furious than ever before.

At last, Peter arrived at the warehouse.

He landed on the far wall. The thief was stunned.

And that's when Spider-Man sprung into action!

The crook's hat flew from his head and Peter finally took a good look at him. Peter felt a heavy weight in his chest. It couldn't be. But it was. The man who had killed his uncle was the same man he allowed to escape into the lift at the studio.

If only Peter had stopped him then! If only he had not acted so selfishly!

Stunned, Peter tied up the criminal in webbing and dangled him off a streetlamp for the police to find. The most Peter could do now was prevent him from hurting anyone else. Through the haze of his grief, Peter realized something. He had not chosen these abilities, but it was his obligation to use them for good.

It was not about money or fame or any of the other rewards his power could give him. He had finally realized that what his Uncle Ben had told him was true:

with great power comes great responsibility.

And that was the rule that Peter Parker lived by from that day forwards.

MARVEL

THE COURAGEOUS CAPTAIN AMERICA™

AN ORIGIN STORY

Before you were born – in fact, long before even the oldest person you know had been born – a peaceful little island sat right off the mainland of a place that was called different things by all the different nations of people who lived there.

As time went on, more and more people came to this little island.

They wanted to leave behind the lives they led in a place they called the Old World ...

... and build new ones in a place where they believed anything was possible.

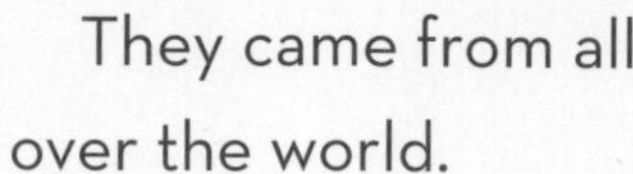
They came from all over the world.

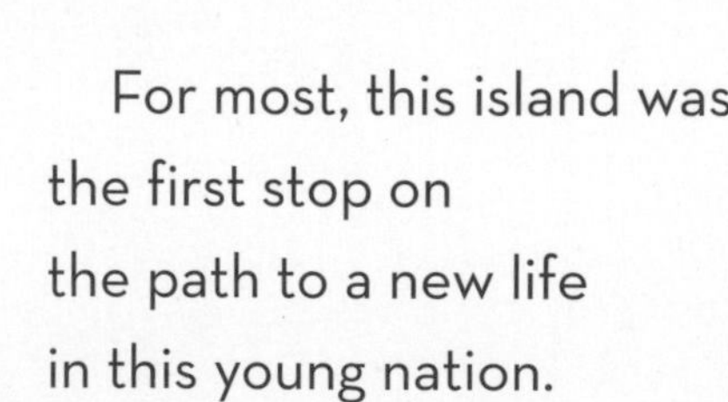
For most, this island was the first stop on the path to a new life in this young nation.

This island was known as Manhattan, in the city of New York.

The country would be known as the United States of America – or America, for short.

Before America was even two hundred years old, it was called upon to fight alongside other countries in a terrible war that was destroying the world.

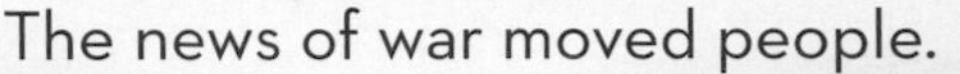

The news of war moved people.

It seemed like everyone in the country wanted to join the army to help.

Including a young man named Steve Rogers.

Steve had been upset about the war for some time. Now that America was involved, he could do something about it.

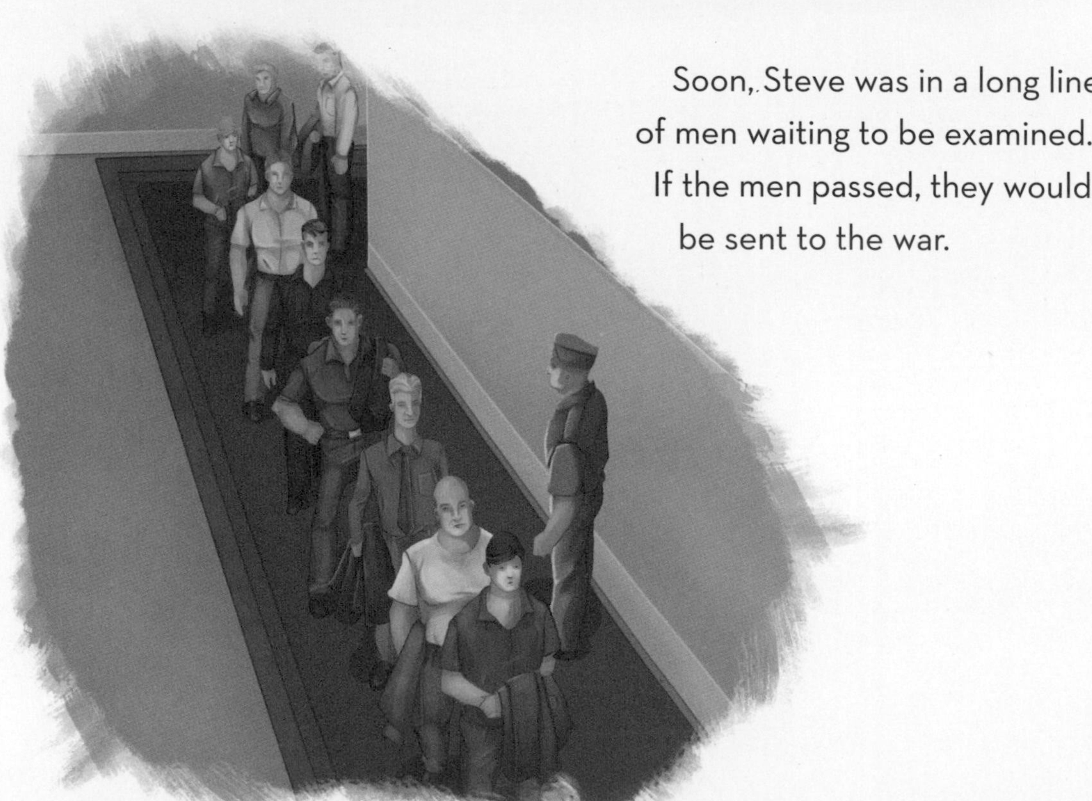

Soon, Steve was in a long line of men waiting to be examined. If the men passed, they would be sent to the war.

Steve waited his turn.

Every man so far had passed.

Steve was confident he would, too.

The doctor told Steve that he was in no shape to join the army.

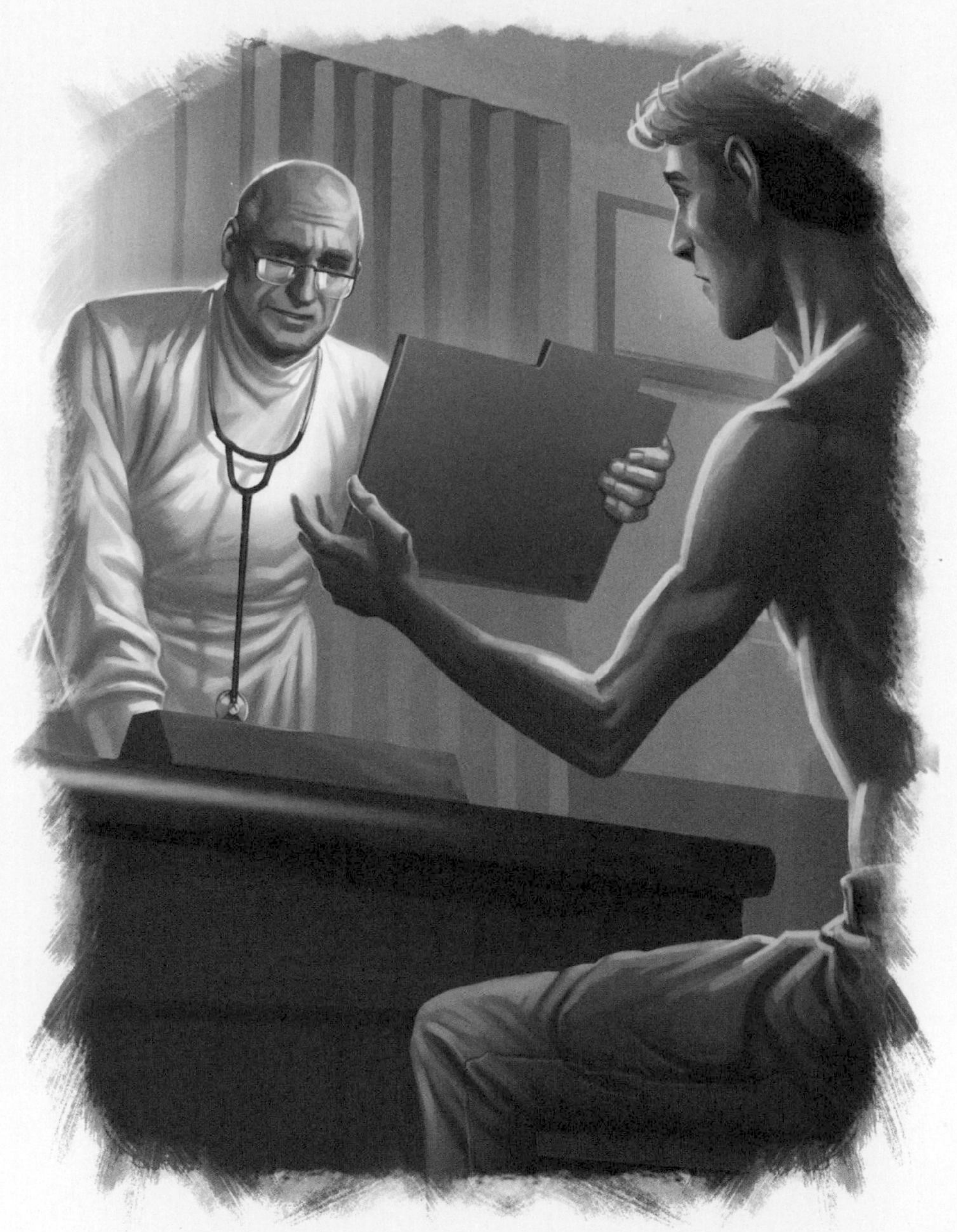

But then he told him there was another way to get into the army. He handed Steve a file marked

CLASSIFIED – PROJECT: REBIRTH.

The doctor told Steve that if the experiment worked, he would be able to join the army.

Steve said he would try anything to become a soldier.

The doctor called in a general named Chester Phillips. General Phillips was in charge of Project: Rebirth.

General Phillips introduced Steve to the project's lead scientist, Doctor Erskine.

He told Steve that the Super-Soldier serum ...

... combined with the Vita-Rays ...

... would transform him from frail and sickly into America's FIRST AVENGER!

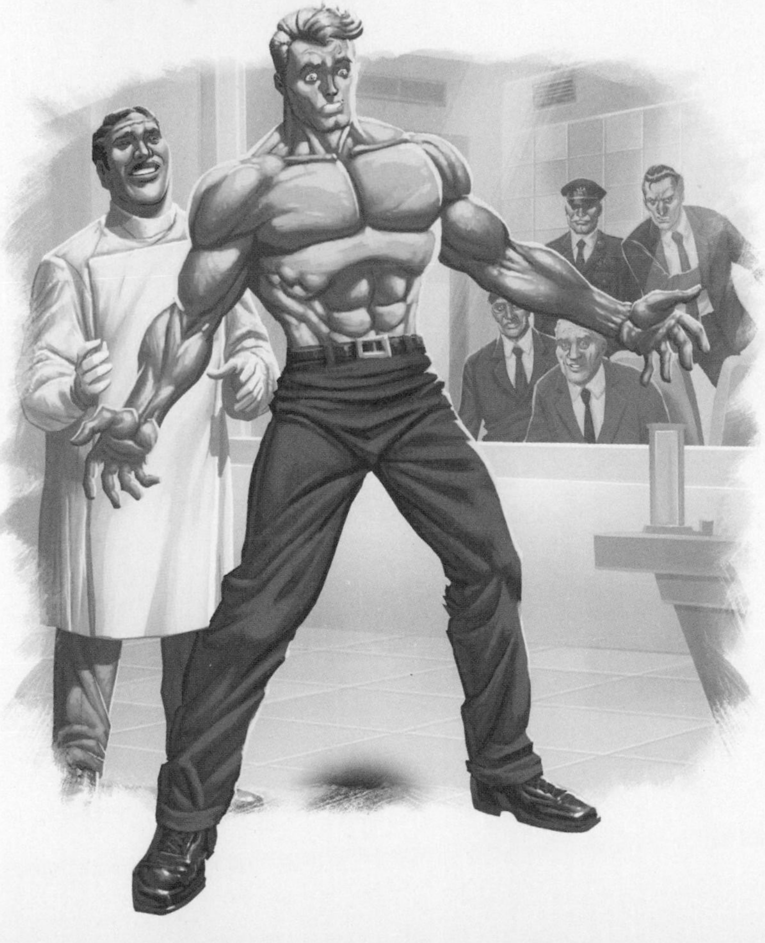

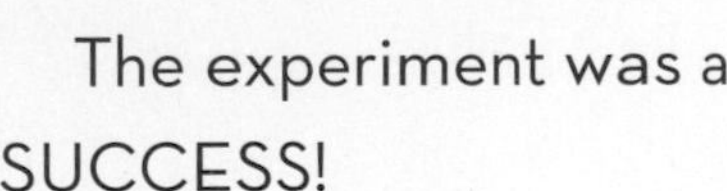

The experiment was a SUCCESS!

But before Steve, General Phillips or anyone else in the lab could notice, an enemy spy who had been working in the lab attacked!

He did not want the Americans to have such power!

The doctor was hurt and unable to duplicate the serum.

But Steve, in his new Super-Soldier body, was safe.

AND HE WAS ANGRY!

The army put Steve through a very special training camp to teach him how to use his new body.

The general presented Steve with a special shield made of the strongest metal known and a unique costume to help Steve mask his identity.

With the costume and shield, Steve would now be known as America's most powerful soldier ...

CAPTAIN AMERICA!

Captain America's missions were often dangerous.

In order to keep his secret safe, the general asked Steve to pretend to be a clumsy army private.

But when no one was looking, Steve donned his costume and fought for justice.

Steve's reputation as a clumsy guy meant he was often transferred.

But Steve's moving around allowed Captain America to fight on many different fronts of the worldwide war!

No one ever suspected that the worst private in the US Army was also the best soldier that the army had!

Captain America kept on fighting for liberty, until finally ...

THE WAR HAD BEEN WON.

Though the country might not always live up to its promises, as long as Steve was able, he vowed to protect it and its ideals: justice, equality, freedom ...

... and the dream of what the nation he loved could accomplish.

Colour and complete these amazing activity pages, then turn to page 161 to find the answers.

Electro is attacking Times Square!

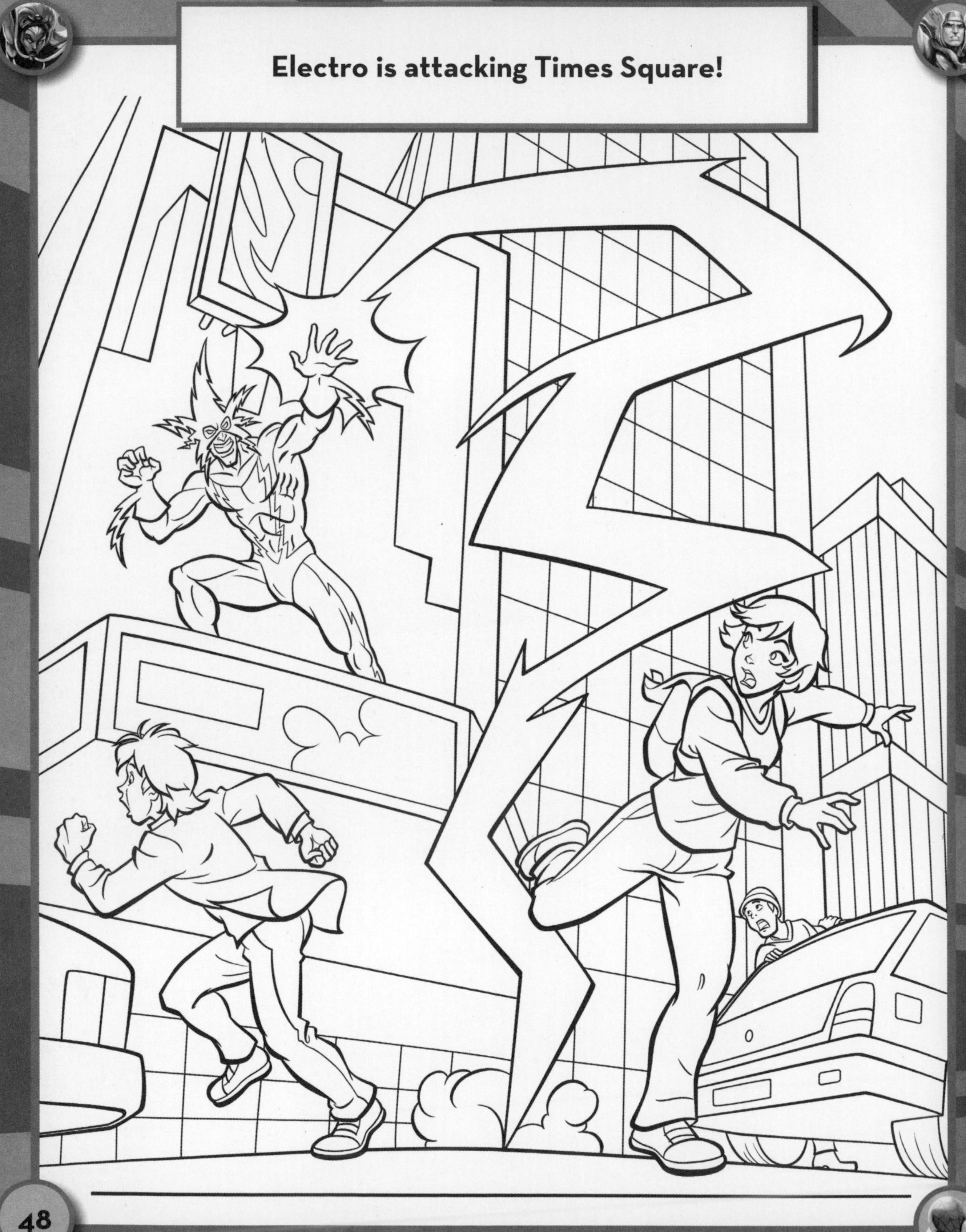

Draw a line from each villain to the picture that best matches his powers.

1. 

A.

2. 

B.

3. 

C.

4. 

D.

5. 

E.

Help Spider-Man work his way through the crowd to find Electro.

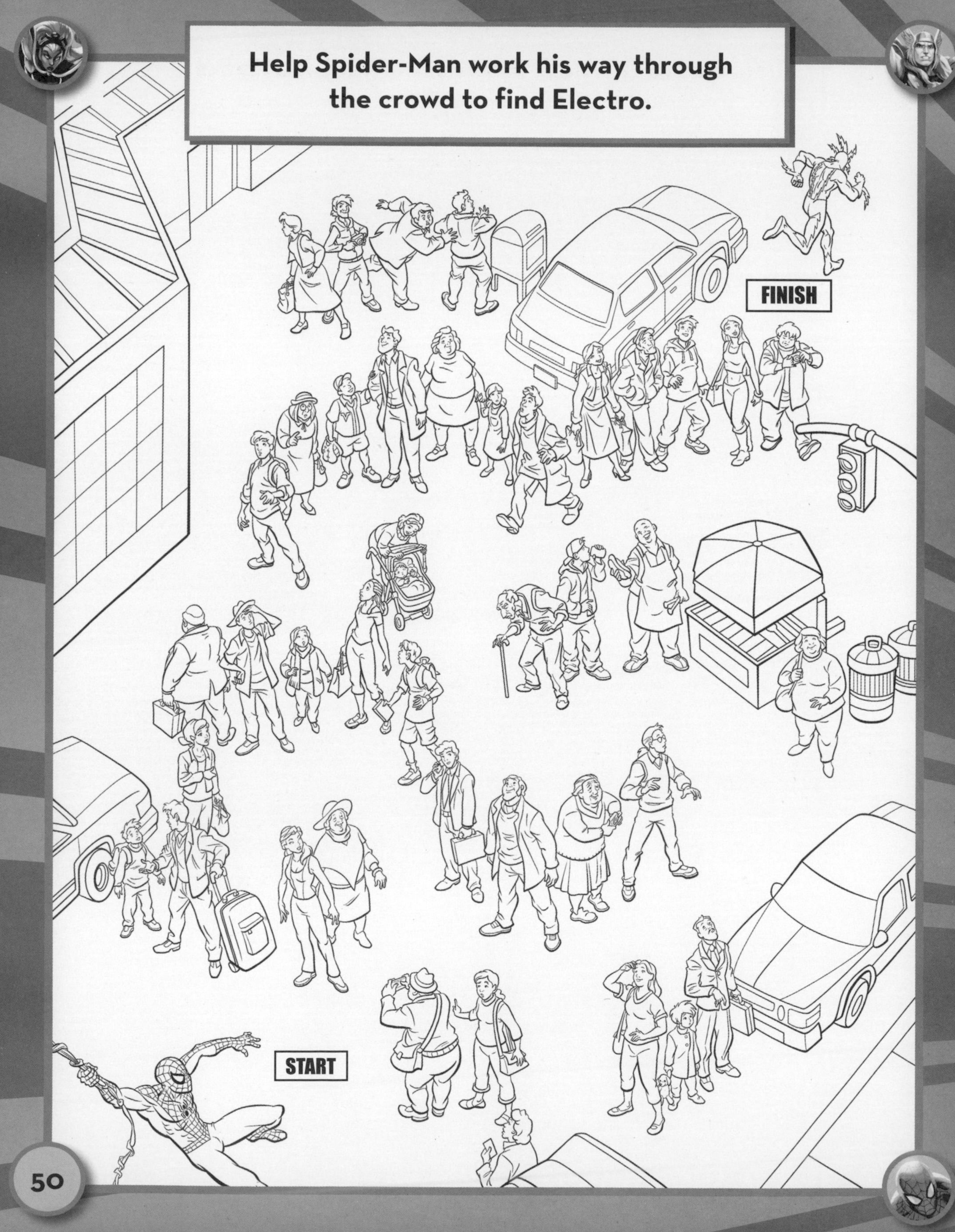

Connect to the dots to see how Electro attacks.

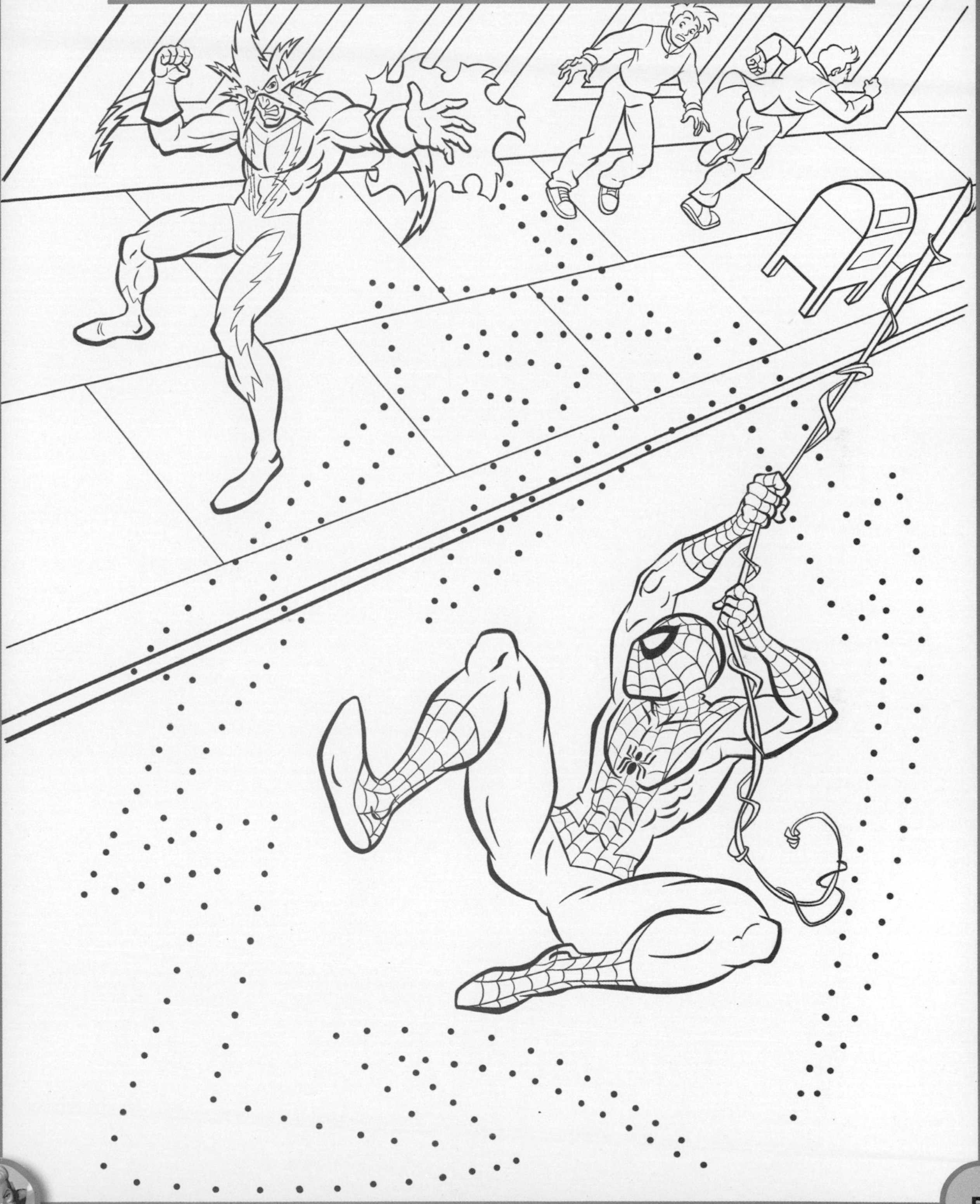

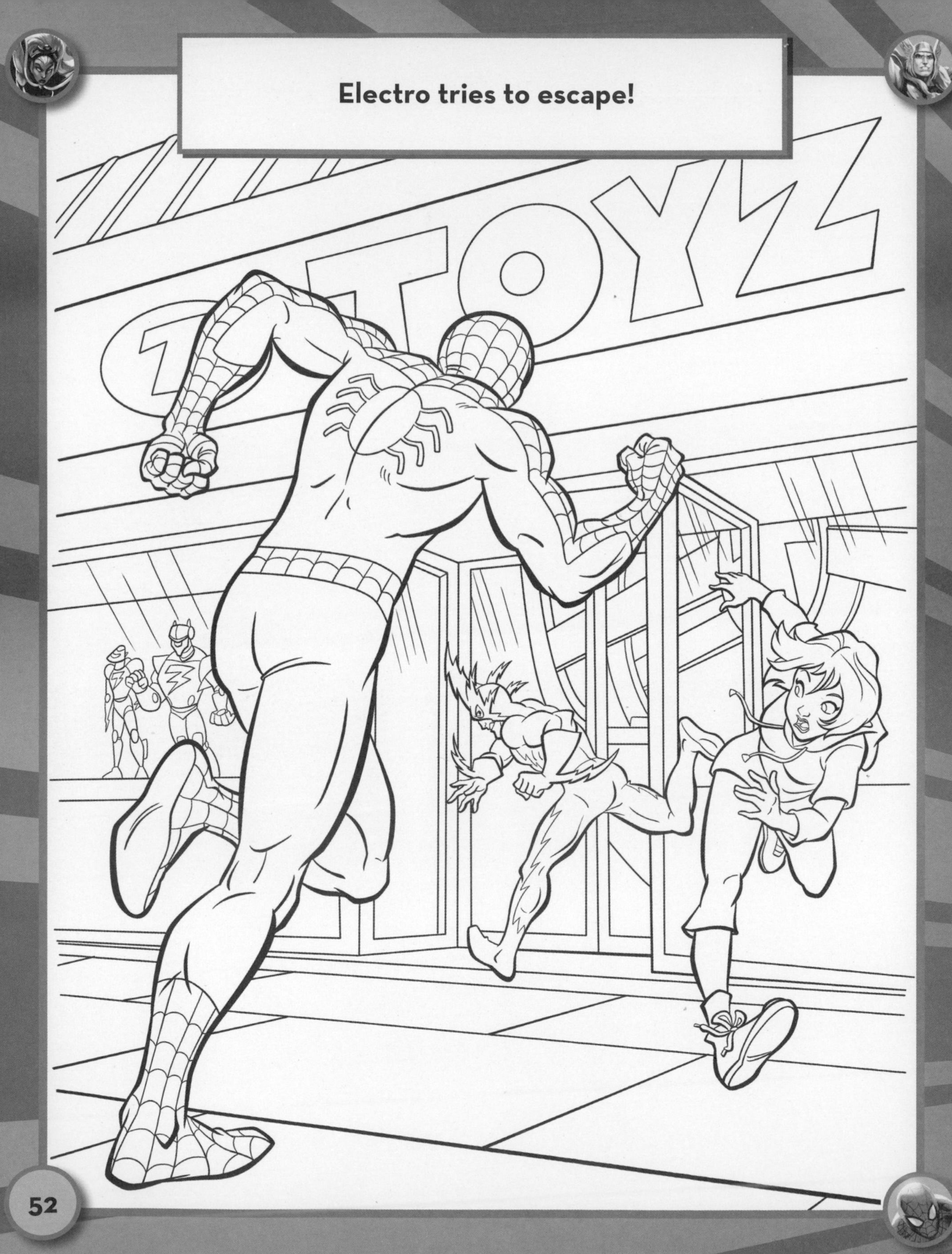
Electro tries to escape!
TOYZ

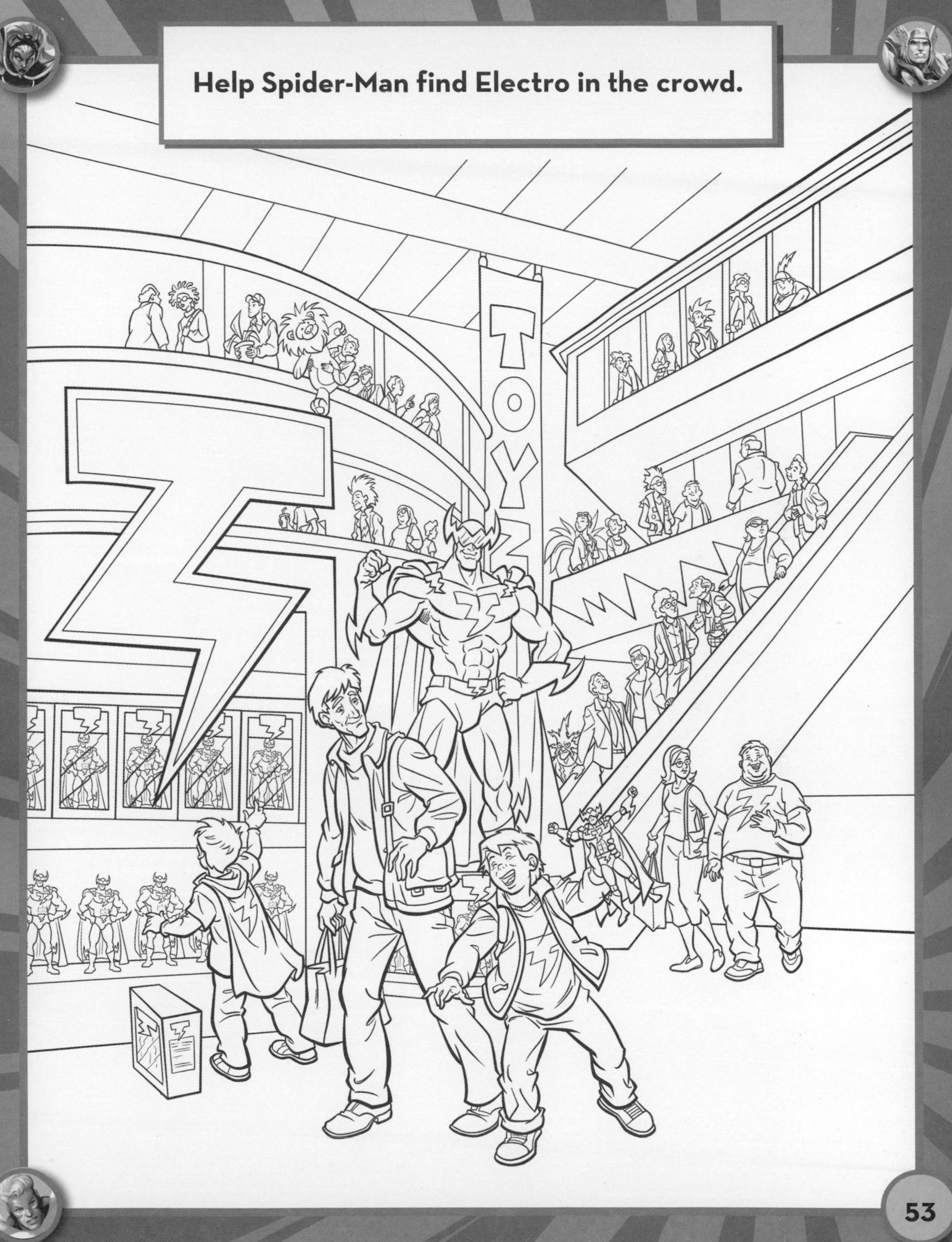
Help Spider-Man find Electro in the crowd.
TOY

Electro decides it's lights out for the toy store!

TOYZ

Which shadow is the real Electro?

1.

2.

4.

3.

Spider-Man turns on his belt spotlight to find Electro. Circle the Spidey symbol that looks like his mask.

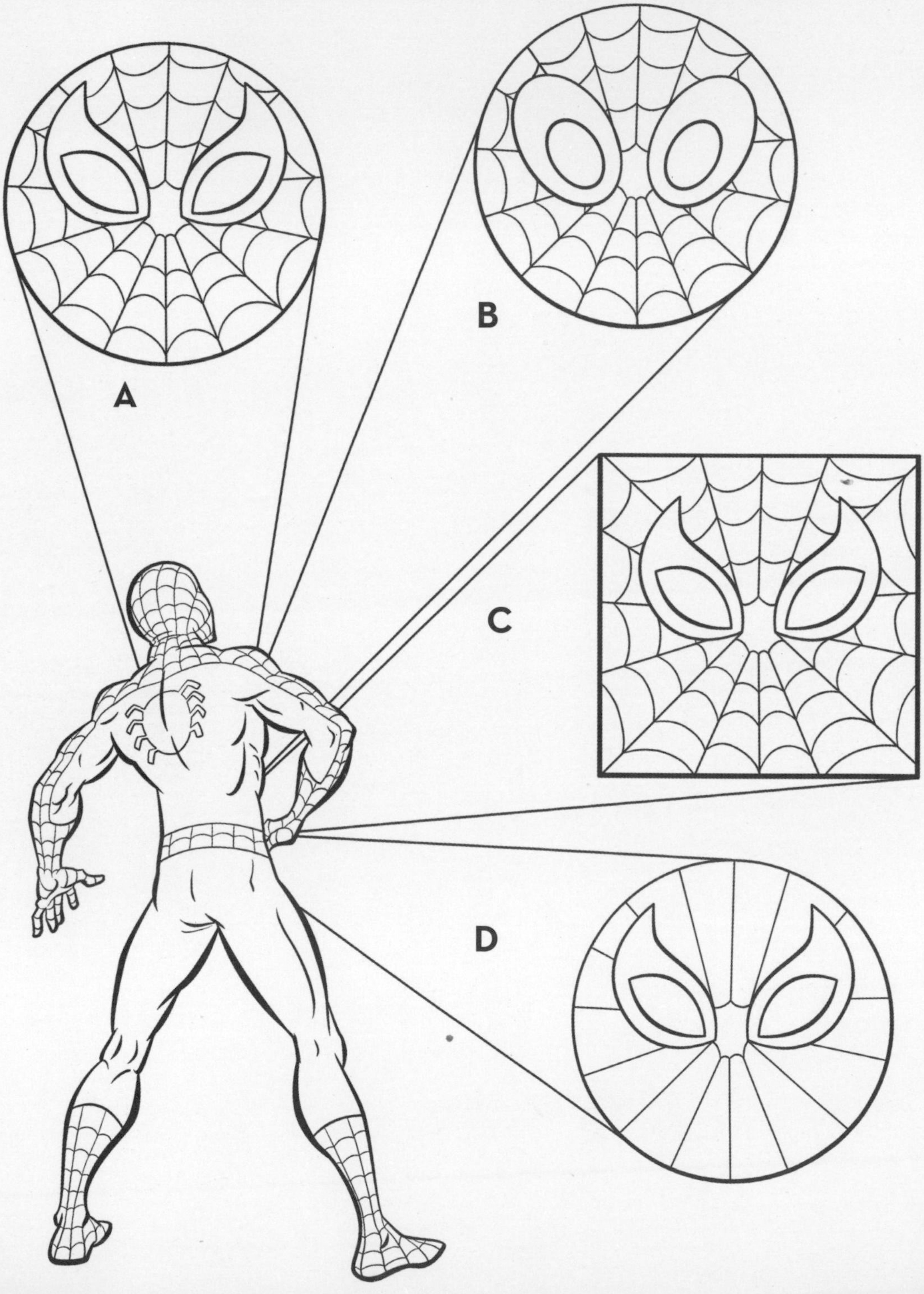

A

B

C

D

**Help Spidey snag Electro with his web-shooter.
Circle the right web!**

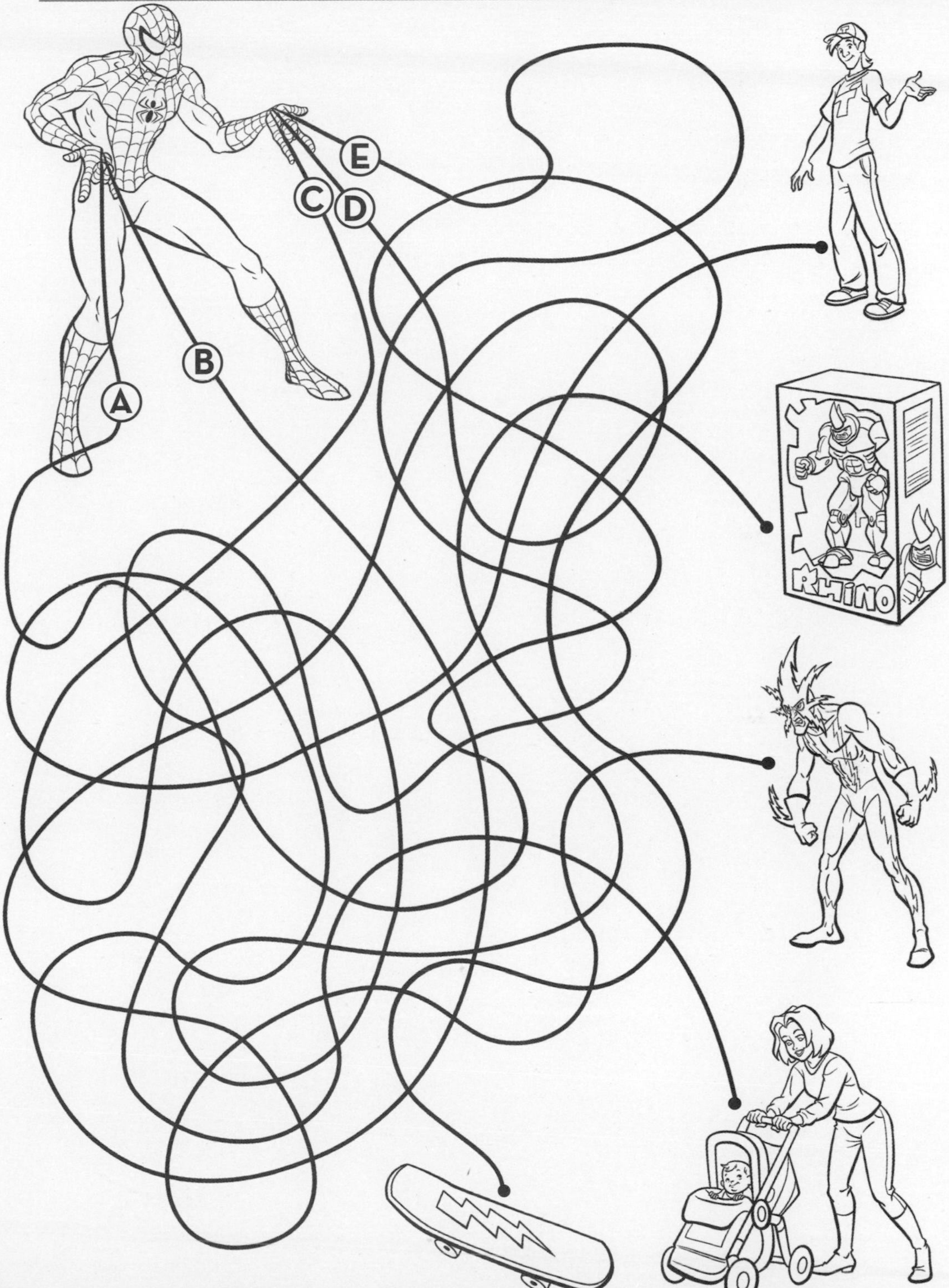

A
B
C
D
E

RHINO

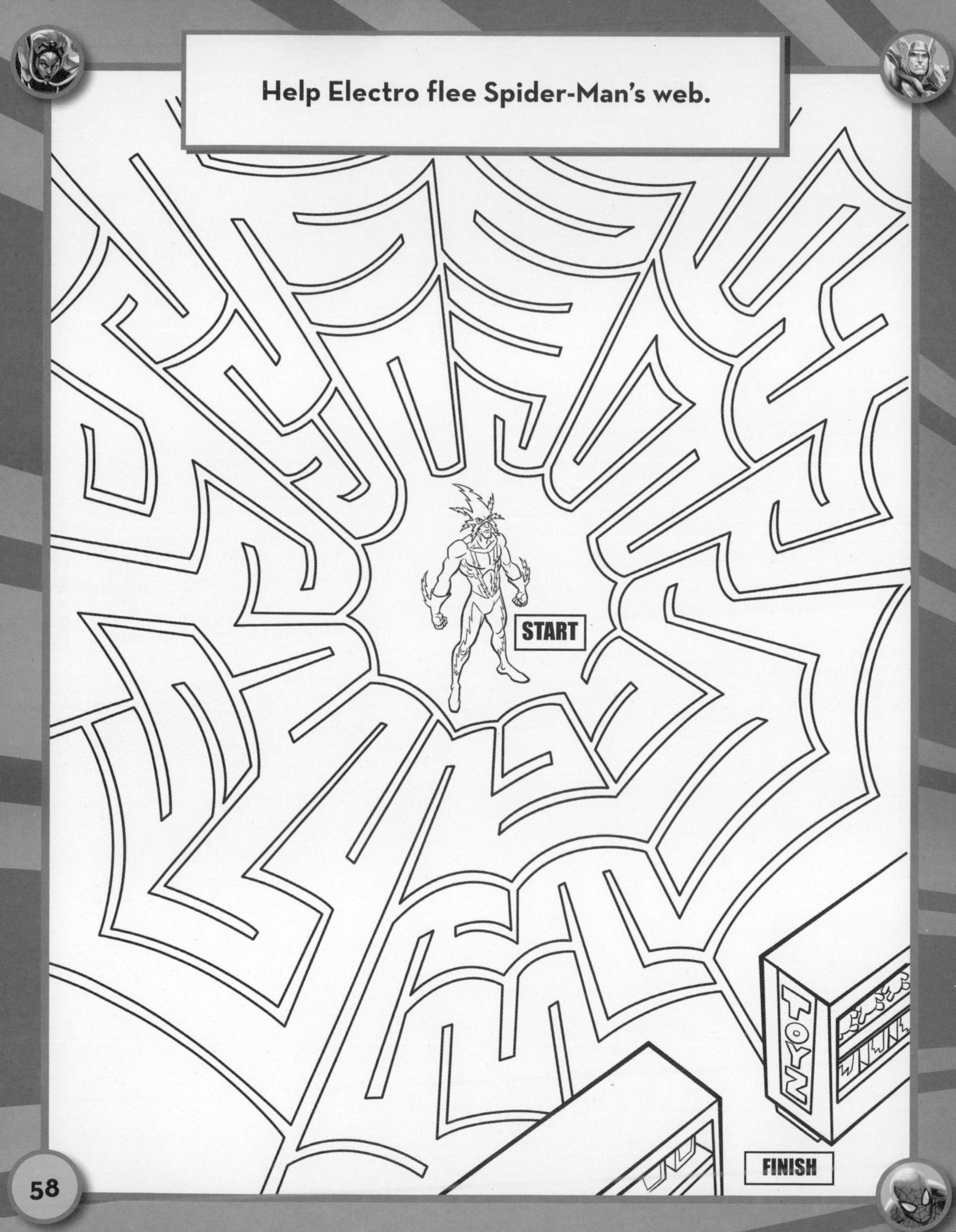
Help Electro flee Spider-Man's web.
START
TOYZ
FINISH

It’s hard to outrun a web-slinger!

Can you spot five things on this page that are different from the last page? Circle them.

A high-stakes struggle on the ferris wheel!

Circle the toy that Spider-Man would like the most.

A

B

C

D

E

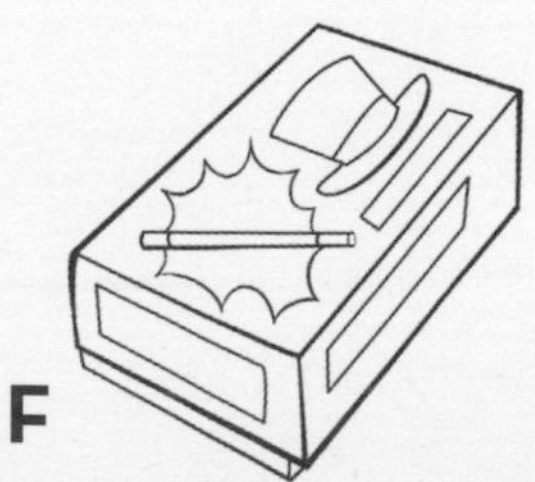
F

Connect the dots to see what trips up Electro!
TOYS

Web-spinning is the fastest way to travel!
DAILY BUGLE

© MARVEL

Help Spidey get to the Daily Bugle.
START
FINISH
DAILY BUGLE

How many words can you spell using the letters in THE DAILY BUGLE?

THE DAILY BUGLE

Leg

Time for a quick change to Peter Parker!

Peter almost missed a button! Which choice is the correct Spider-Man symbol? Circle it.

A

B

C

D

E

F

Circle the five things that are different between these two pictures.

Help J. Jonah Jameson finish his crossword puzzle.

ACROSS:

1. *The Daily Bugle*'s ace photographer

2. Short for Doctor Octopus: Doc ____

3. Feline burglar: Black ___

4. Hydro-Man is made up of this

DOWN:

1. Electro has the ability to control this

2. The ___ Goblin

3. Spider-Man's hard-skinned horned foe

1 Across
1 Down
2 Down
3 Down
2 Across
3 Across
4 Across

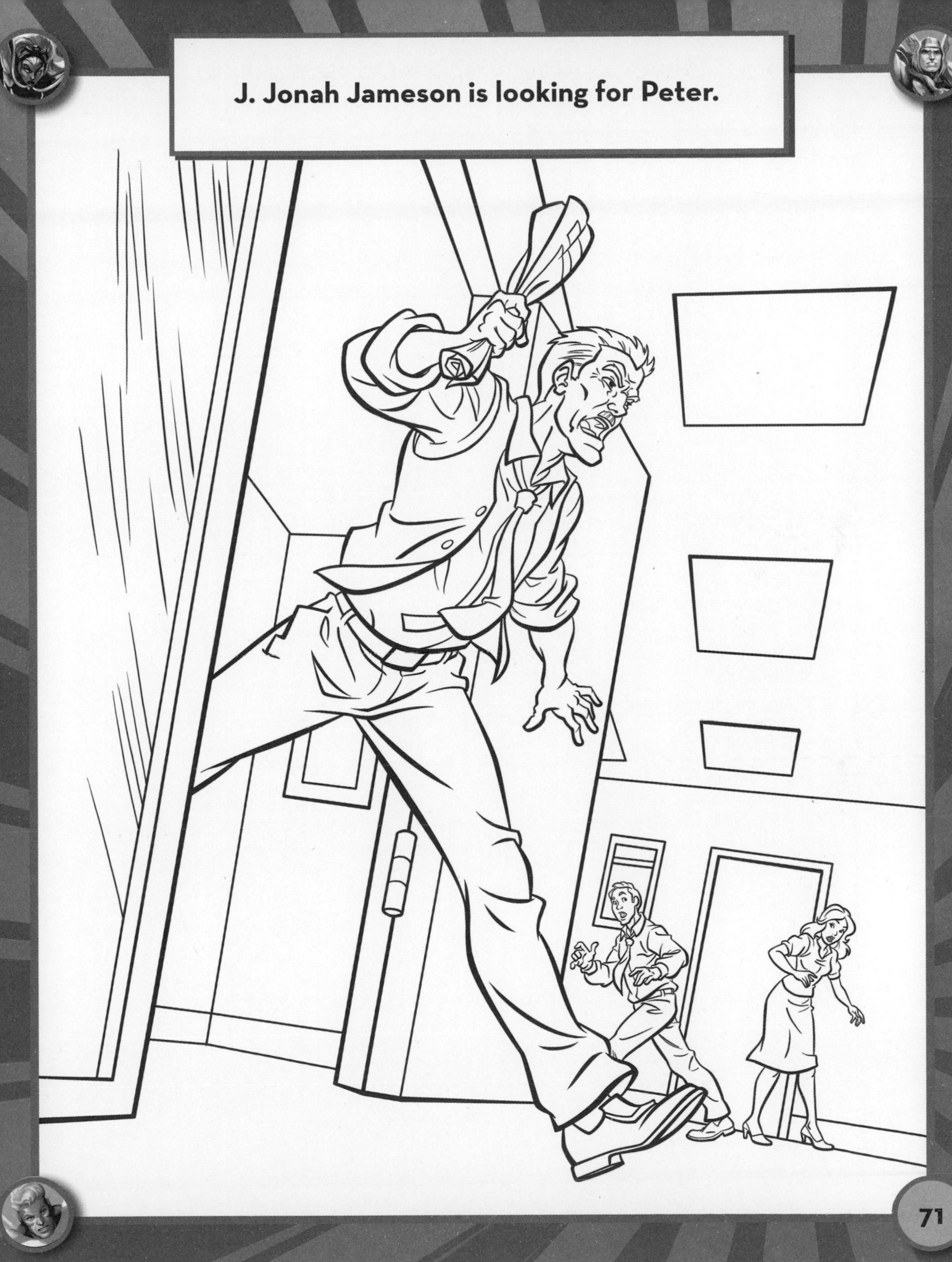
J. Jonah Jameson is looking for Peter.

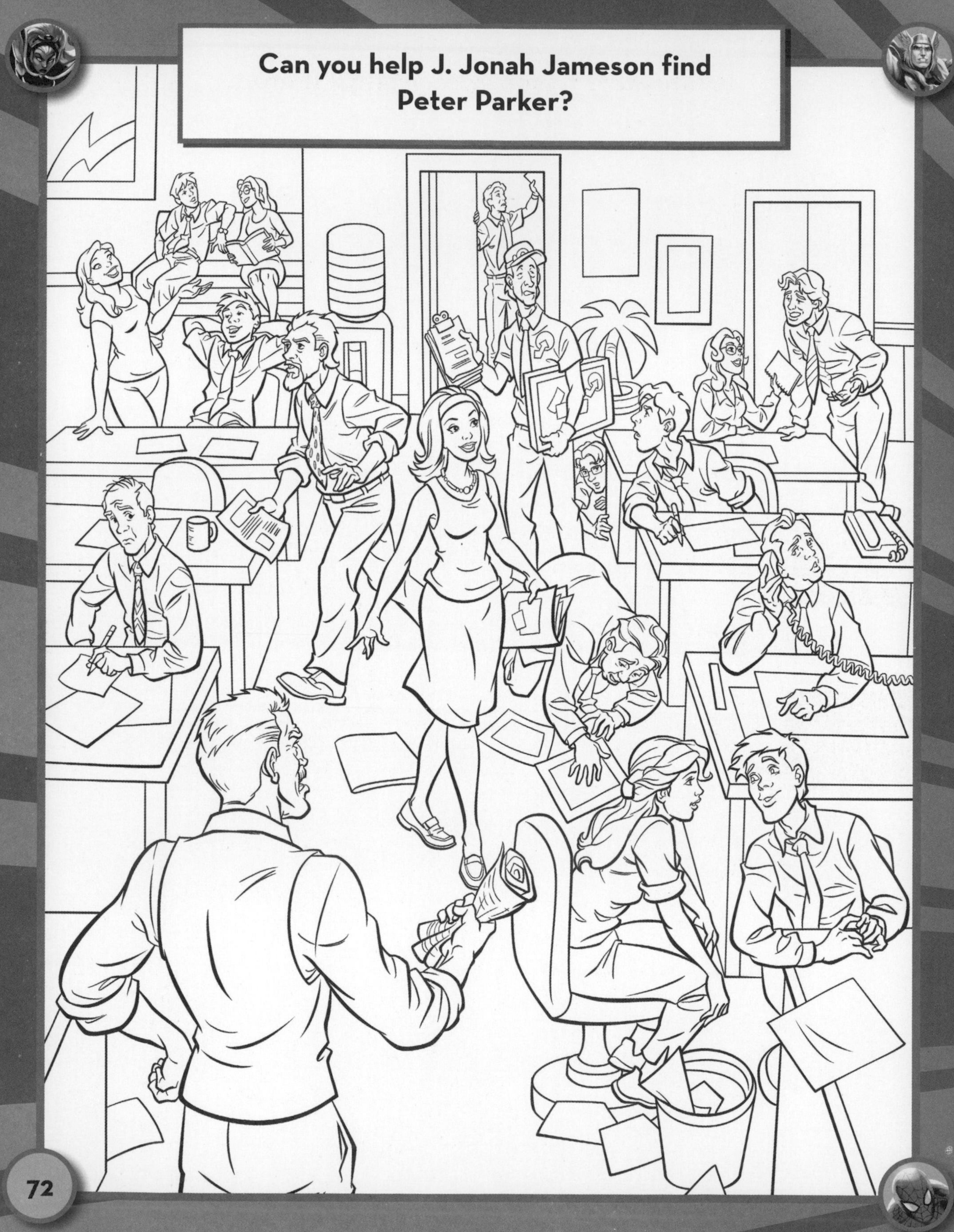
Can you help J. Jonah Jameson find
Peter Parker?

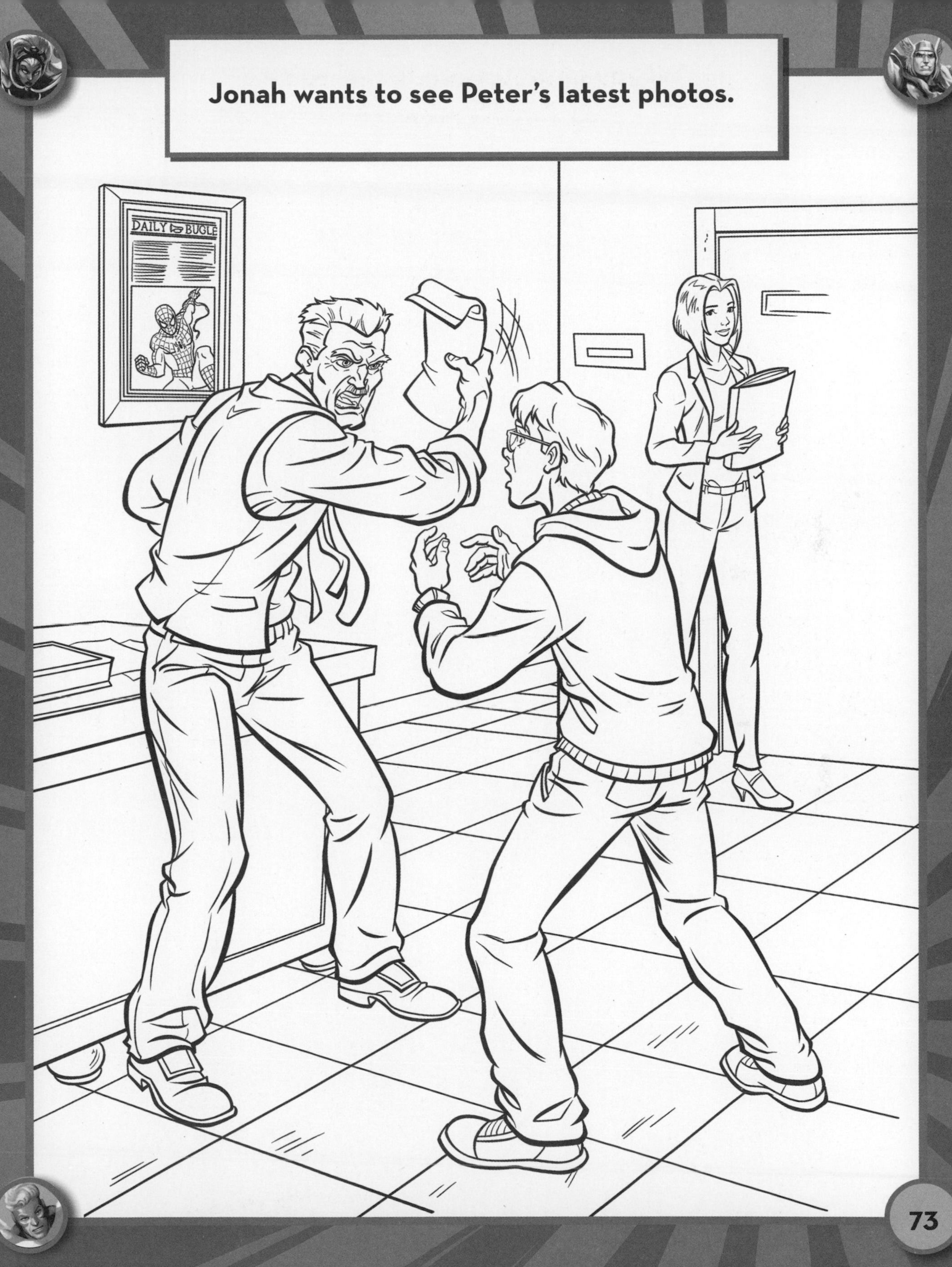

Jonah wants to see Peter's latest photos.

Which photo is exactly the same as Jonah's picture?

A

B

C

D

Mr Jameson likes Peter's photo of Spider-Man fighting a werewolf. Draw the werewolf!

Find these words in the puzzle below. The words can go up, down, backwards, forwards or diagonal.

Chameleon
Hydro-Man
Lizard
May
Morbius
Mysterio
Spider-Man
Venom
Vulture
Webshooter

M	Y	S	T	E	R	I	O	Q	C
Y	V	P	B	G	Z	L	E	N	H
E	L	I	Z	A	I	M	A	Y	A
R	Z	D	C	Z	R	O	D	S	M
U	H	E	A	E	M	R	I	E	E
T	Y	R	F	L	O	B	R	M	L
L	D	M	V	M	R	I	O	N	E
U	R	A	A	U	F	U	P	A	O
V	E	N	O	M	L	S	S	Y	N
R	E	T	O	O	H	S	B	E	W

It's Spider-Man vs. the Lizard.

Which three are Spider-Man's enemies? Circle them.

A

B

C

D

E

F

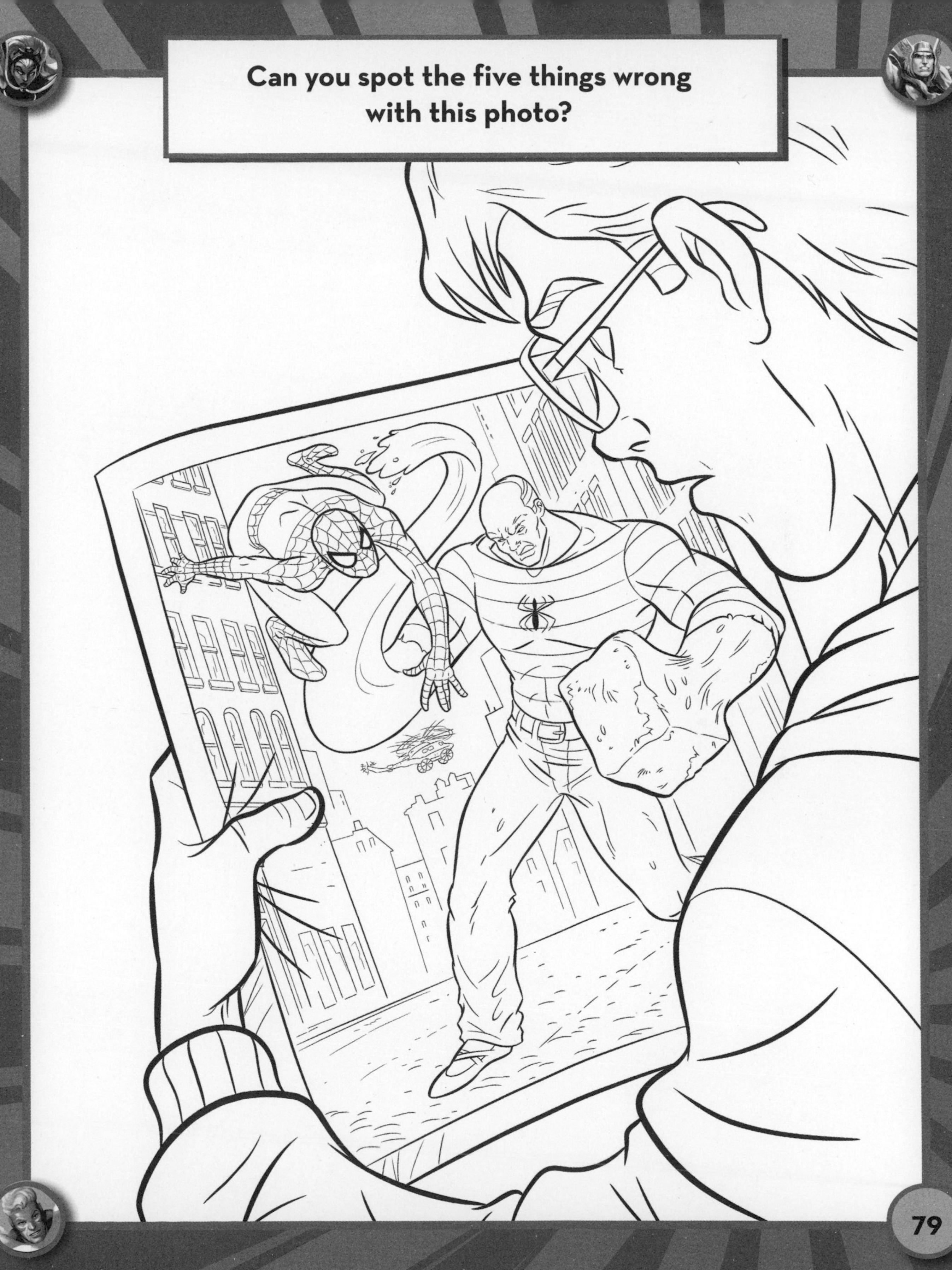
Can you spot the five things wrong with this photo?

It's Spider-Man vs. the Green Goblin.

Help Peter find the correct missing piece of his photograph.

A

B

C

D

E

How many times can you find the word Spidey in the puzzle below? Look up, down, forwards, backwards and diagonally.

S	S	Y	Y	S	S	S
Y	P	E	Y	P	P	P
E	I	I	E	I	D	I
D	D	D	D	D	I	D
I	E	E	I	E	E	E
P	Y	P	P	Y	Y	Y
S	P	I	S	E	Y	S

Peter needs to get back up to the Daily Bugle newsroom. Help him pick the right lift.

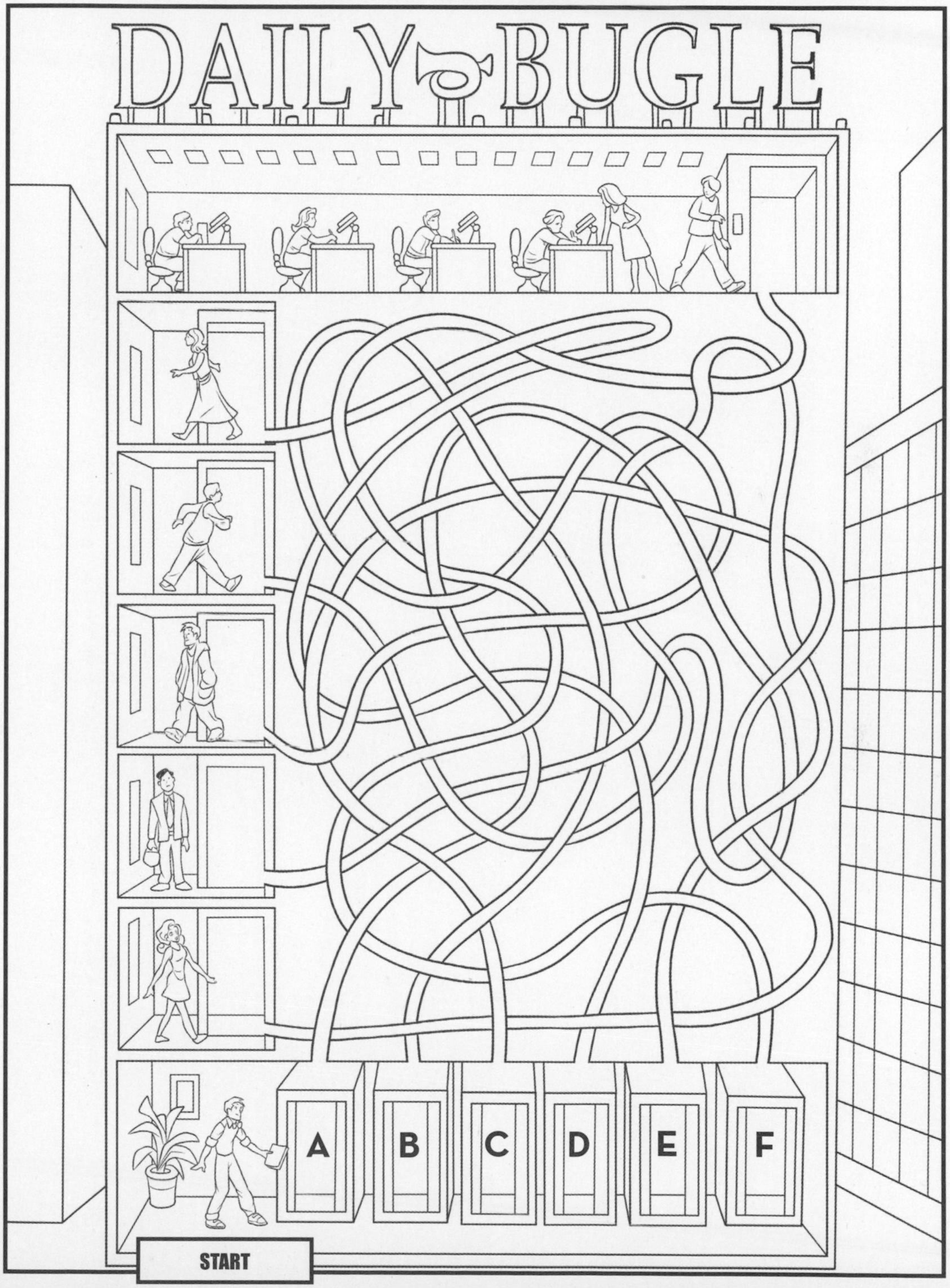

DAILY BUGLE

A B C D E F

START

J. Jonah Jameson decides to buy every photo with Spider-Man in it. How many pictures does he buy?

Help Spidey swing to the open window.
Which web should he choose?

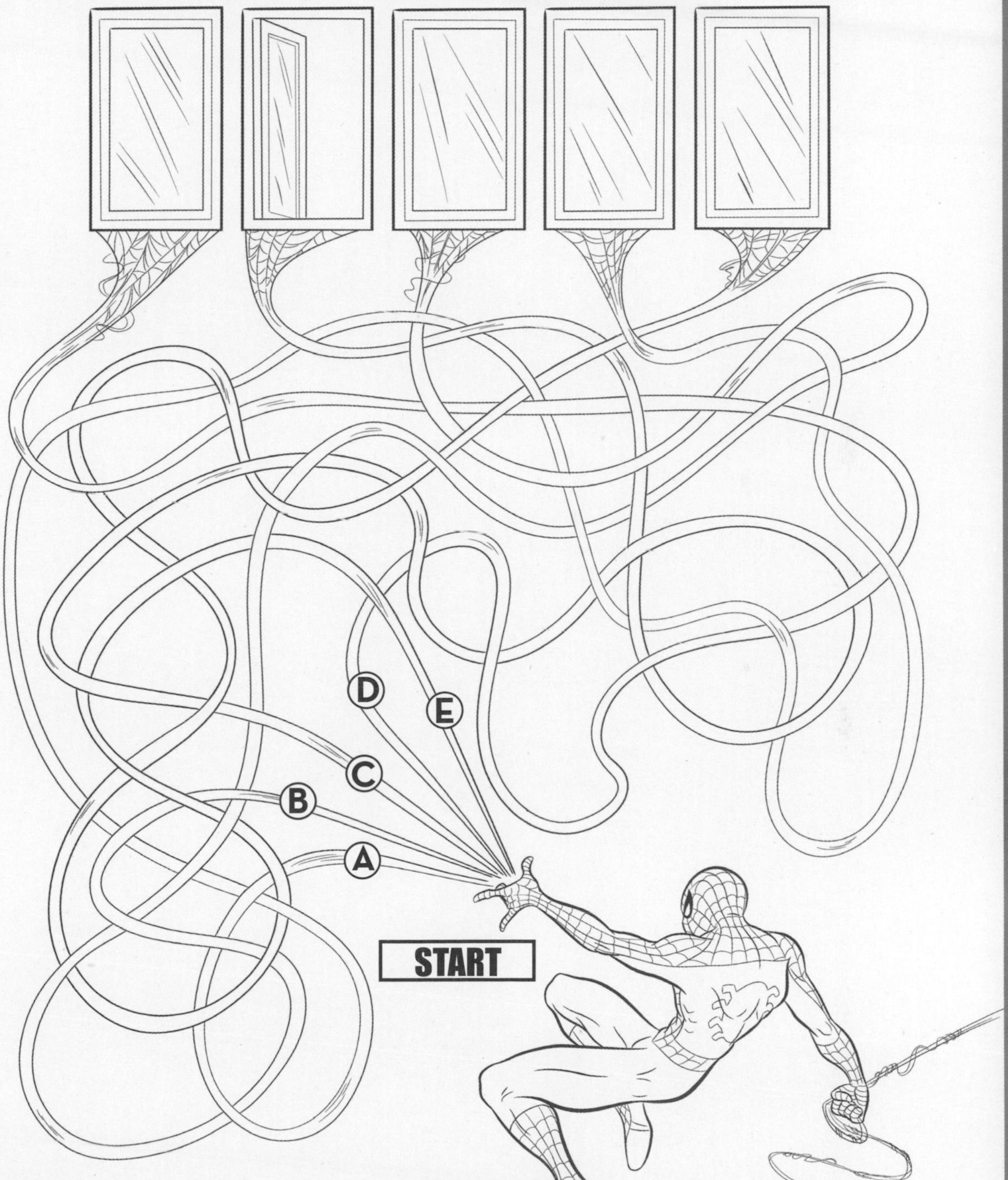

D

E

C

B

A

START

Captain America sprints into battle!

Five trolls have transformed into copies of Captain America. Which Cap is the real one?

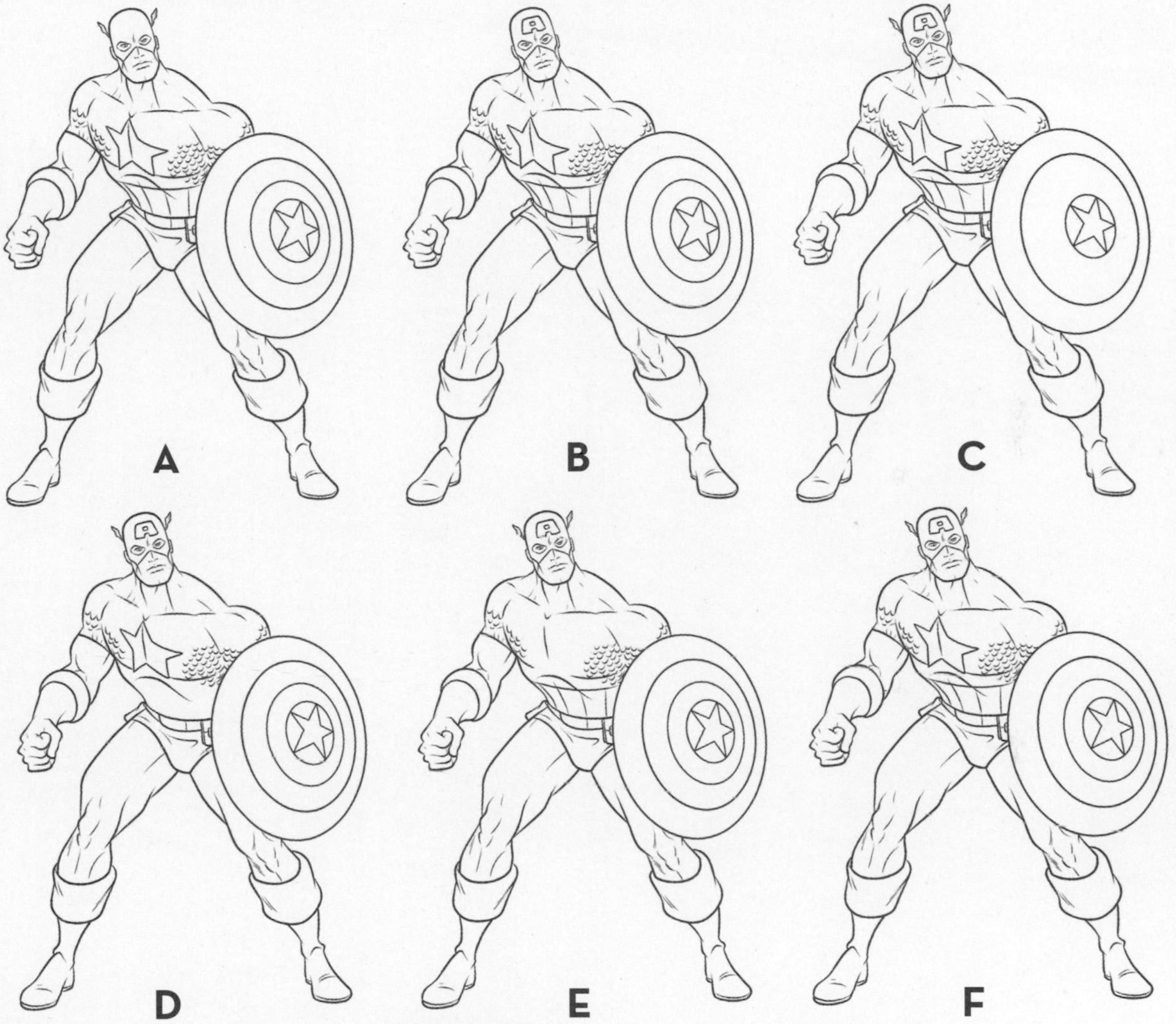

A

B

C

D

E

F

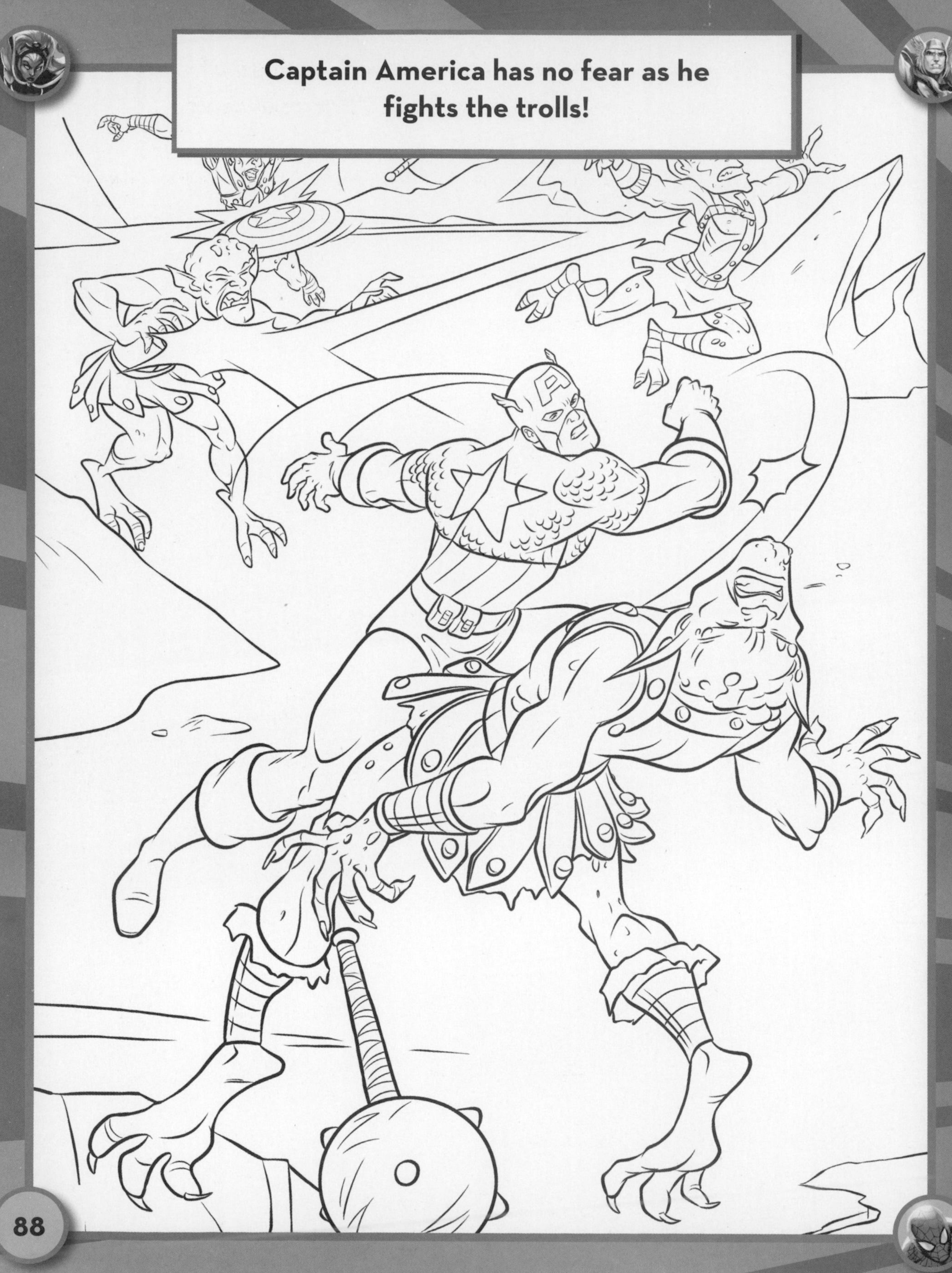
Captain America has no fear as he fights the trolls!

Help the clever Captain America decode the message.

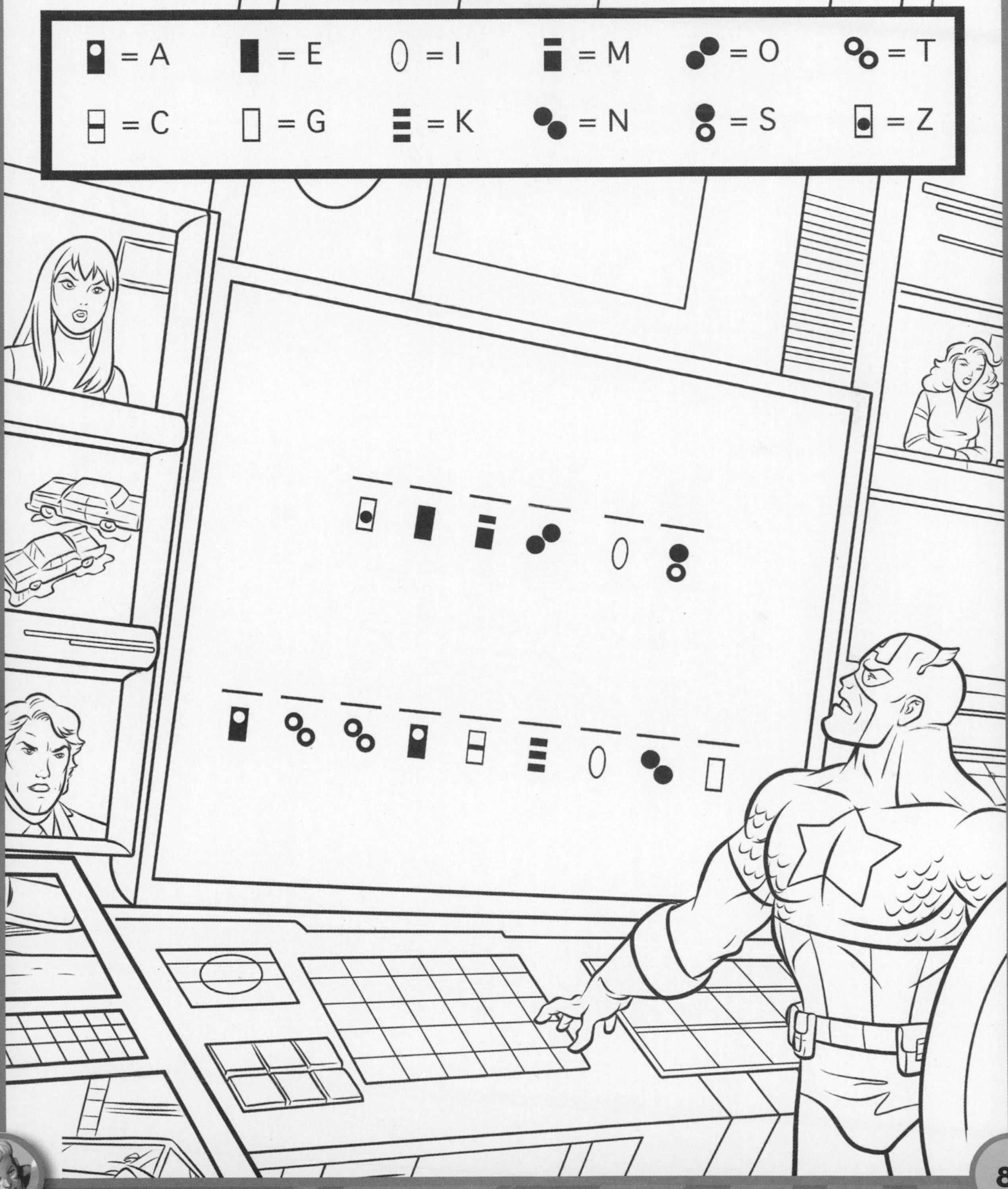

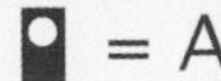

= A = E = I = M = O = T

= C = G = K = N = S = Z

What does Cap call?

Wasp and Ant-Man have come to
Captain America's aid.

Giant Man is a handy hero to have around!

Wield that shield!

Thor leaves his home in Asgard to protect the people of Earth!

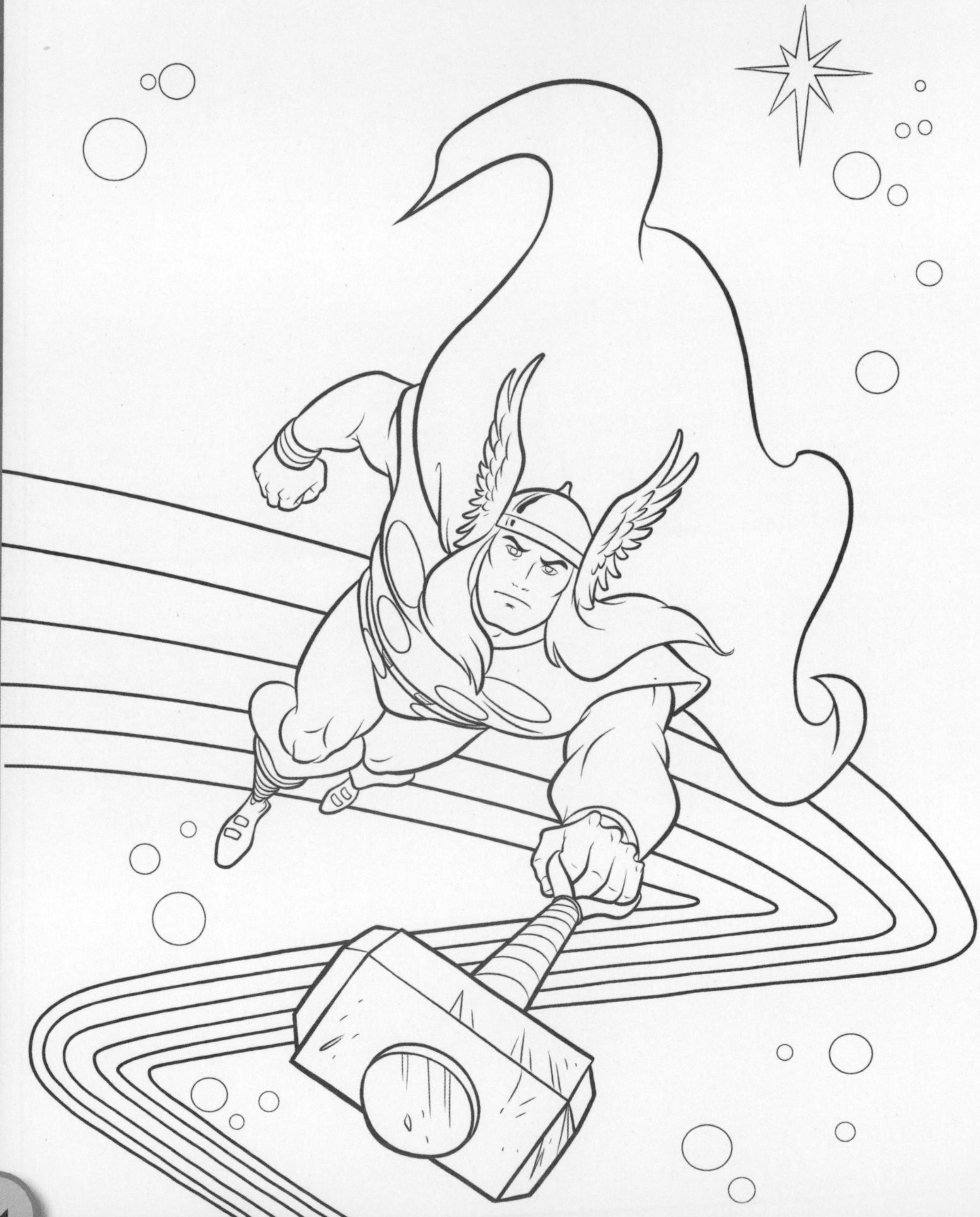

The Mighty Thor arrives in New York!

Find the real name of Thor's hammer!

___ ___ ___ ___ ___ ___ ___

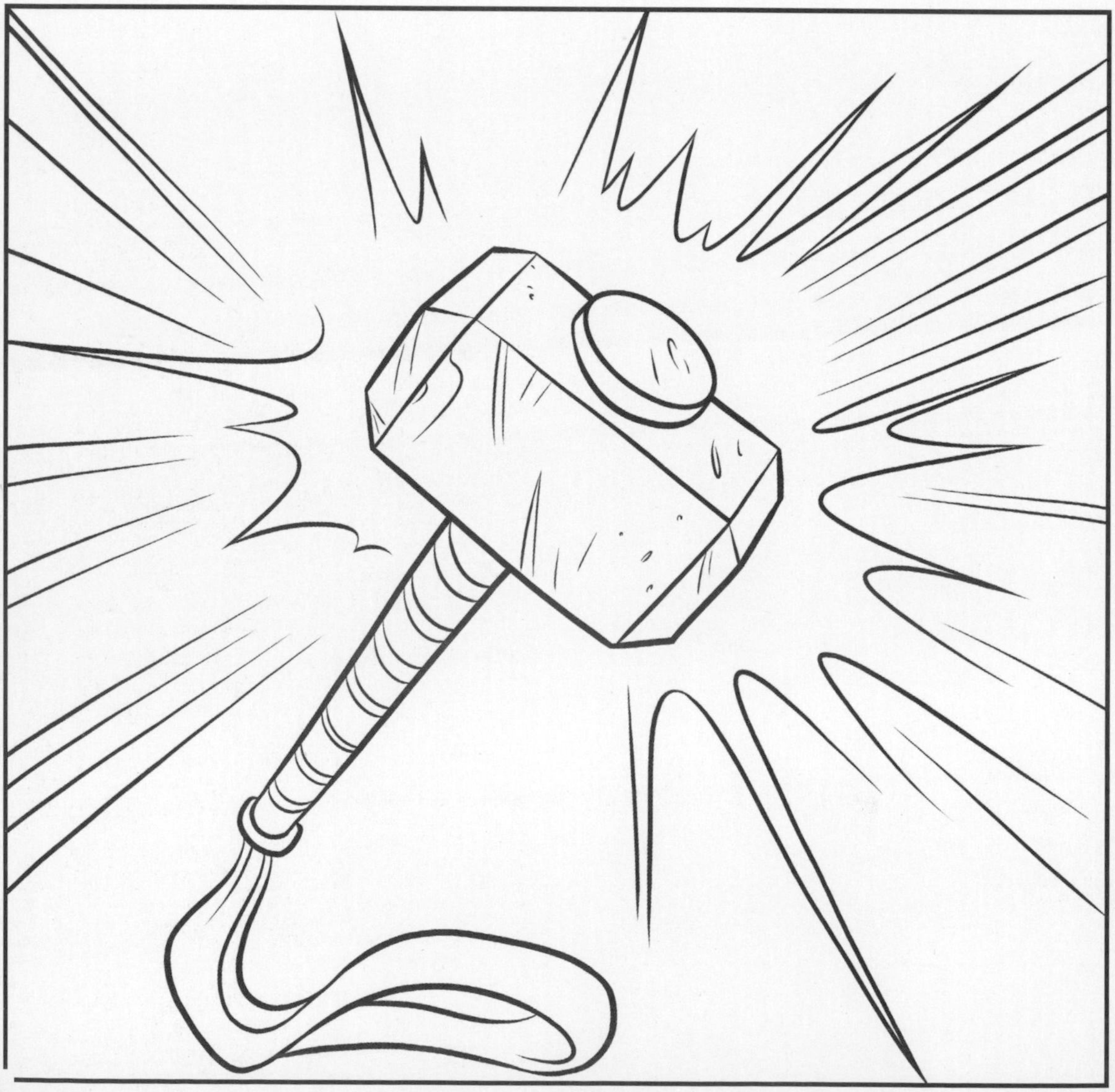

Thor's father Odin rules Asgard!

Thor's evil brother Loki wants to rule Asgard and destroy Thor!

Jealous Loki has made a copy of Odin's Throne. Spot four differences between the real throne on the left and Loki's copy on the right!

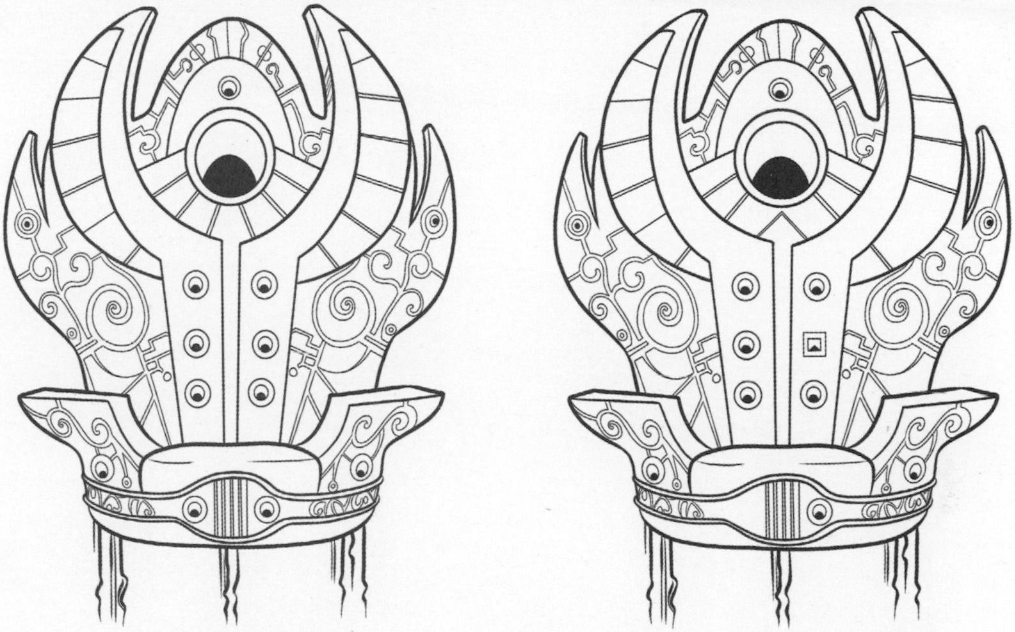

Loki fools Odin with a fake letter from Heimdall, guardian of the rainbow bridge! Find out what the note says!

A T O R L K C

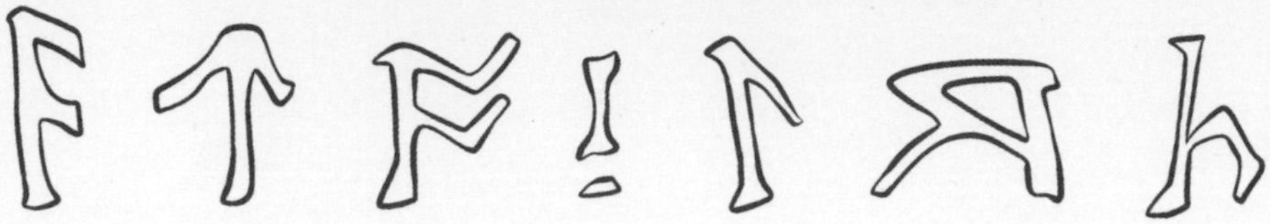

Odin rushes to the Rainbow Bridge, but Heimdall is surprised to see him!

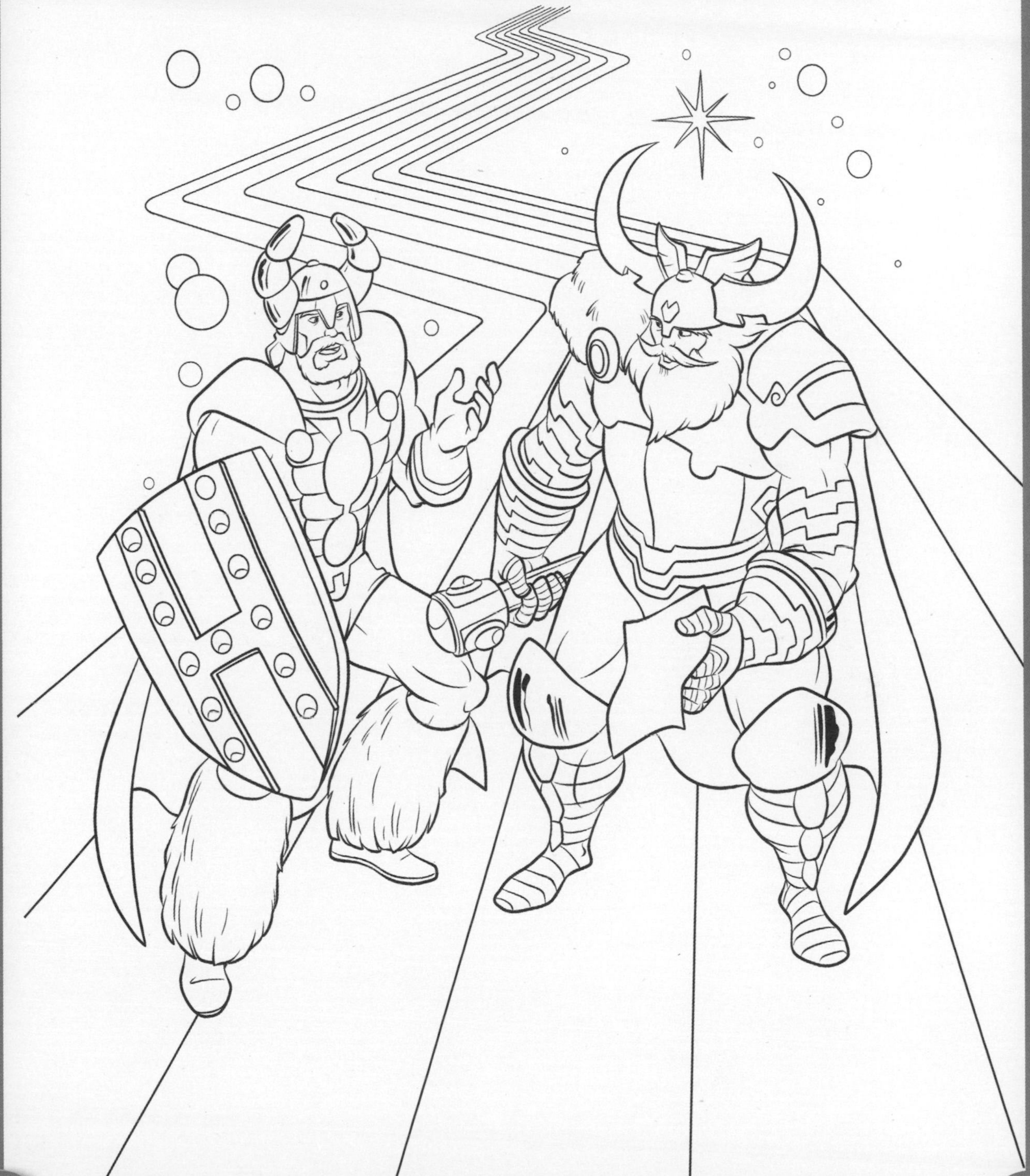

With Odin gone, Loki seizes power in Asgard!

Using magic, Loki frees the Storm Giant and sends him to earth!

Thor flies above the city. Find and circle the Storm Giant to help Thor find the danger that threatens Earth!

The Storm Giant is causing destruction. Find ten differences between the picture of the block before the Storm Giant arrived and the picture of the block after!

BEFORE

AFTER

Meanwhile, in Asgard, Loki frees
The Fire Giant and sends it to Earth!

Thor is trapped between two giants!

Thor throws Mjolnir to Asgard to seek help from his friends!

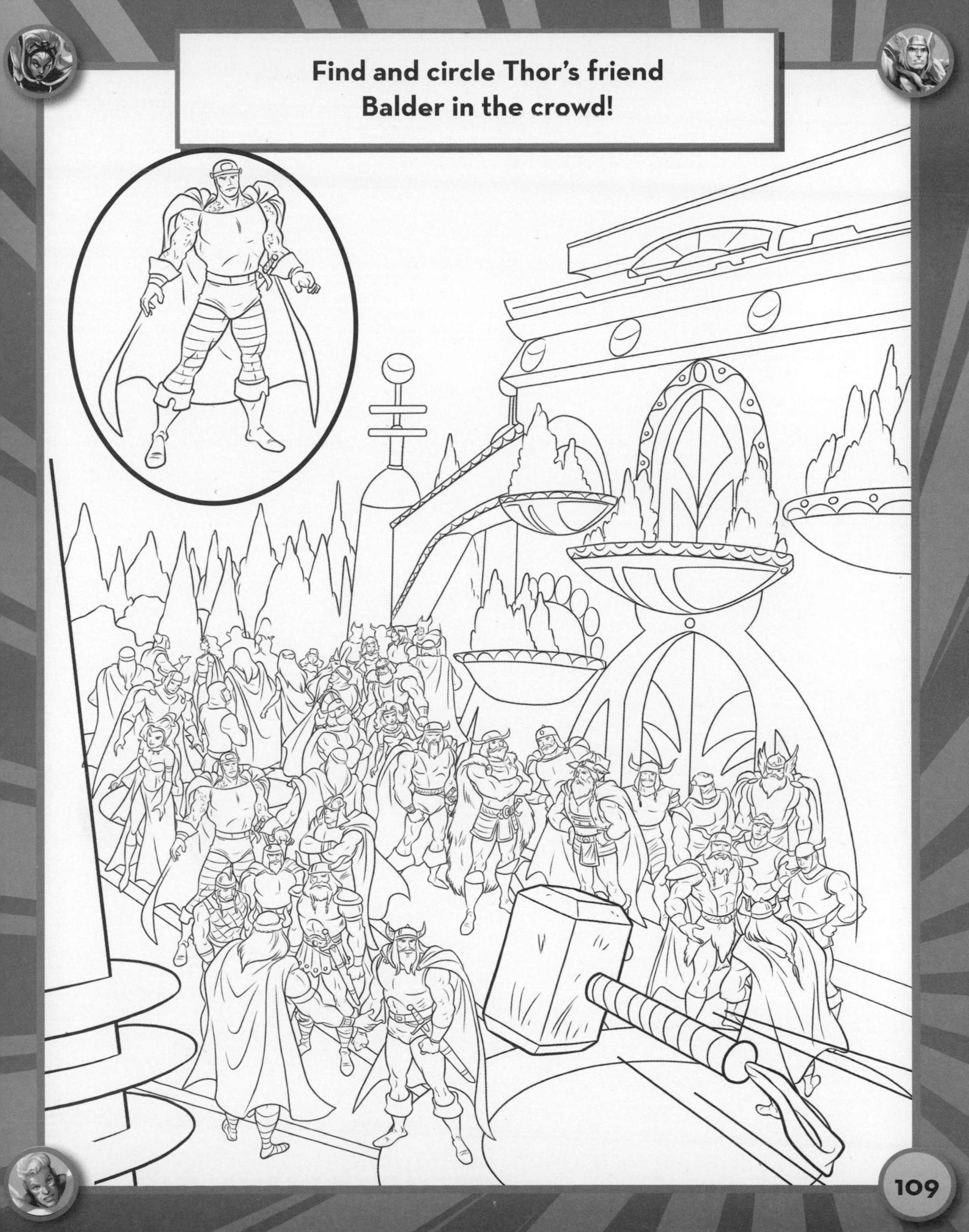
Find and circle Thor's friend
Balder in the crowd!

**Guide Mjolnir to Thor's other friends,
The Warriors Three, by tracing a path through Asgard!**

Thor's friends are ready to help!
Match each one to his battle gear!

A

B

C

D

1

2

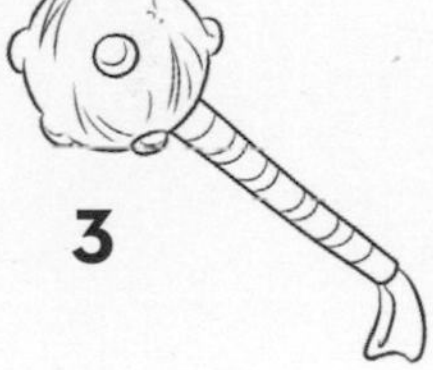

3

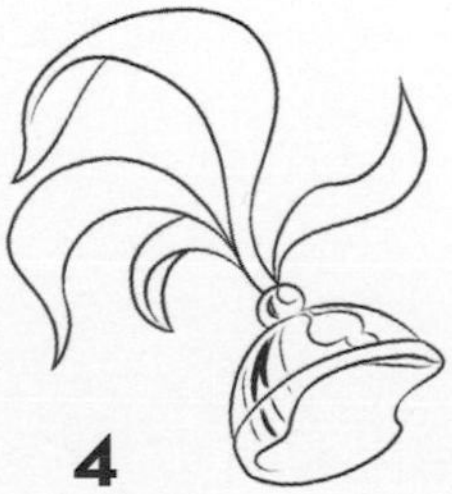

4

Balder the Brave rides to Thor's aid!

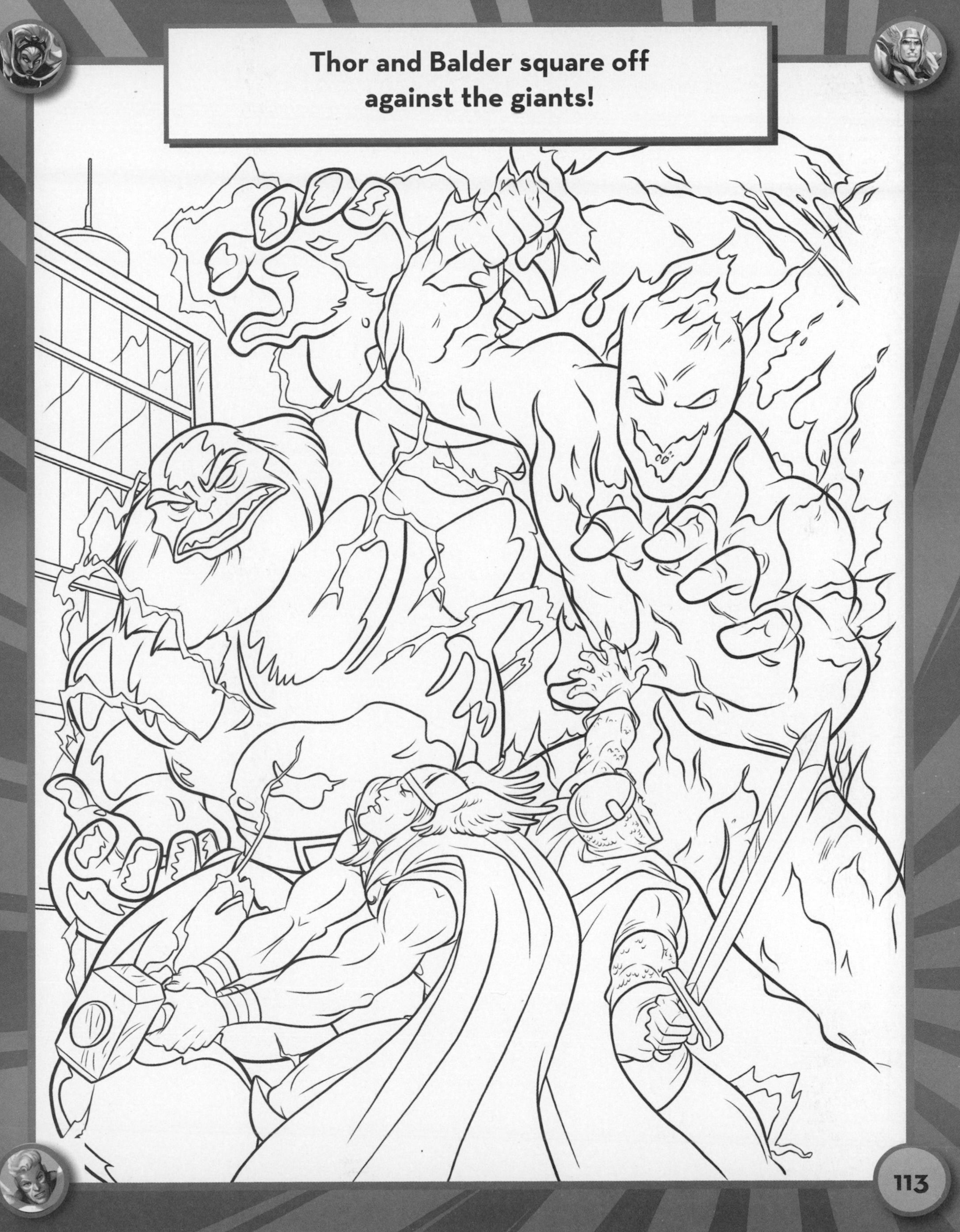
Thor and Balder square off
against the giants!

Balder is in trouble!

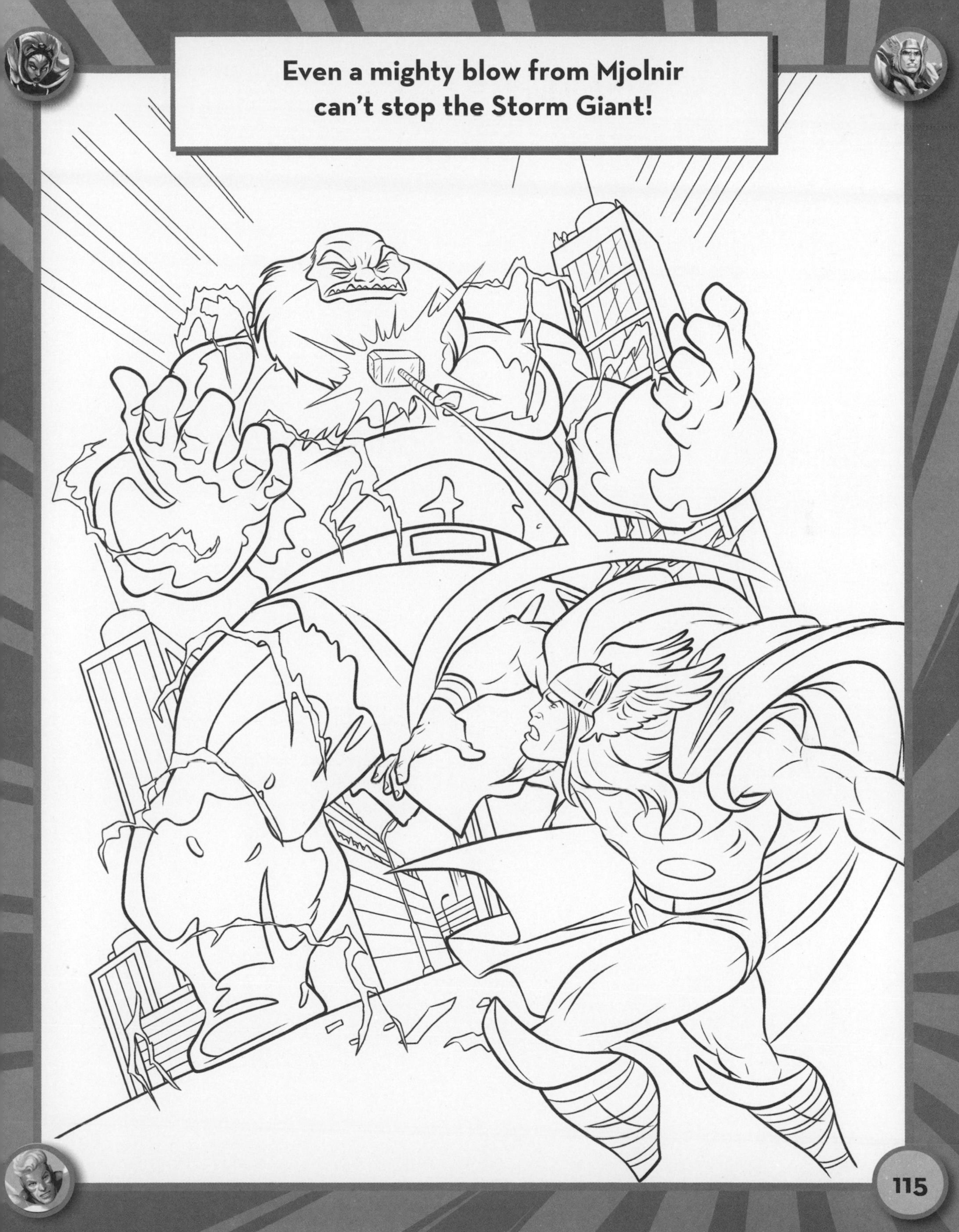
Even a mighty blow from Mjolnir
can't stop the Storm Giant!

The Storm Giant strikes! Replace each letter in the message with the letter that comes before it in the alphabet to find out why Thor is not afraid!
GPPM! UIPS DPNNBOET UIF MJHIUOJOH!
_ _ _ _ _! _ _ _ _ _ _ _ _ _ _ _ _ _ _ _
_ _ _
_ _ _ _ _ _ _ _ _ _ _!

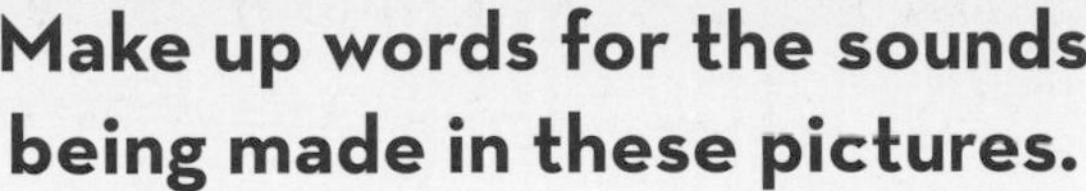

Make up words for the sounds being made in these pictures.

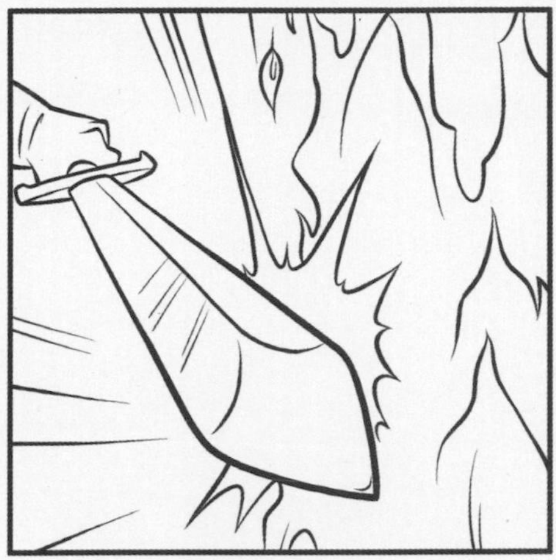

THWACK!

Thor's lightning strike stuns the
Storm Giant ...

... and Mjolnir finishes the job!

With one enemy defeated,
Thor races to help Balder!

Thor tells Balder the Fire Giant's weakness. Decode his message to Balder.

A E H S T W R

__ __

__ __ __ __ __

__ __ __ __ __!

Thor and Balder lead the Fire Giant to the harbour!

The Fire Giant swings at Balder ...

... while the Mighty Thor strikes from behind!

The Fire Giant falls into the harbour!
Write the sound effect for the Fire
Giant's fall into the water!

With the Giants defeated, Thor and Balder return them to Asgard.

Which path will lead Thor and Balder to Asgard?

FINISH

A B C

START

Meanwhile, in Asgard, Odin has discovered
Loki's trick and Loki is in trouble!

Odin exiles Loki and the Giants!

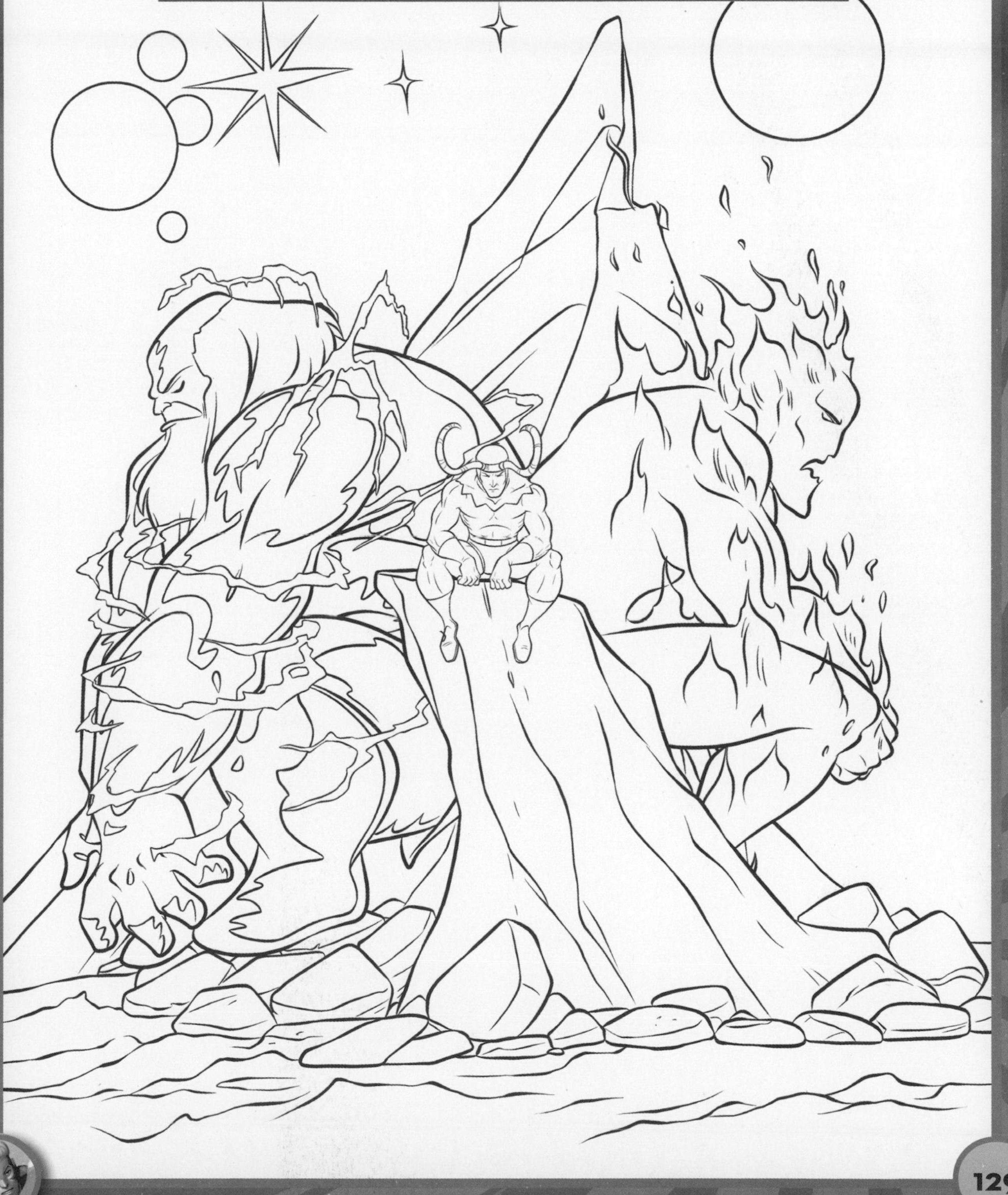

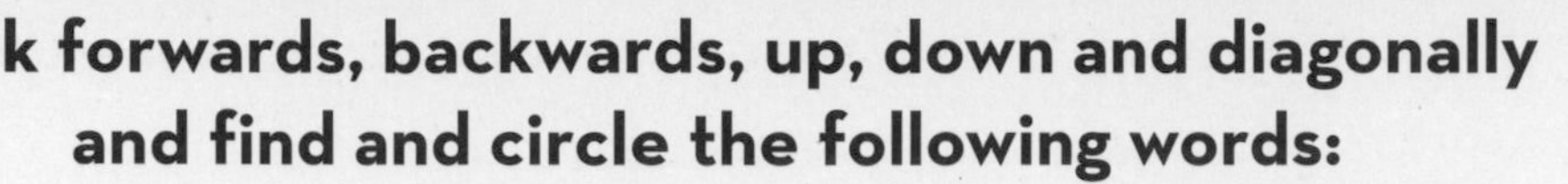

THOR, ODIN, LOKI, BALDER, HOGUN, VOLSTAGG, FANDRAL

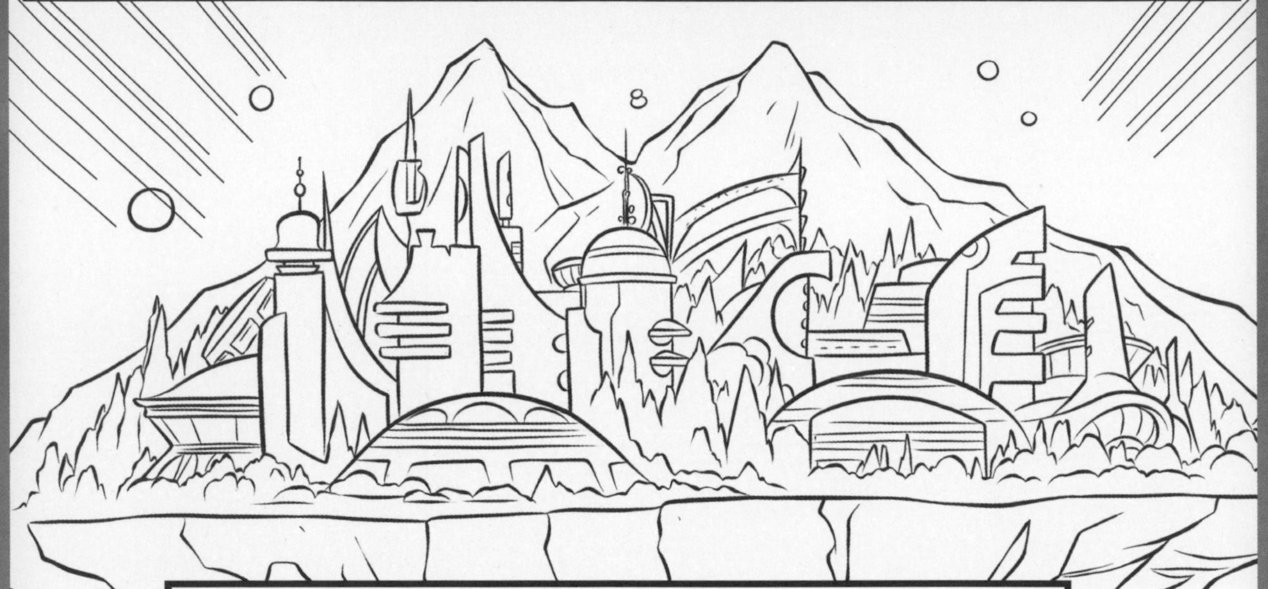

G	T	H	O	R	I	D	I
L	G	B	D	E	J	K	S
J	M	A	I	B	O	U	L
K	B	L	T	L	I	N	P
O	M	D	O	S	T	I	N
I	D	E	R	T	L	D	O
R	E	R	N	U	G	O	H
F	A	N	D	R	A	L	V

Professor X tells Cyclops about some dangerous mutant activity in New York City. Unscramble the clues to discover where the X-Men are needed.

1.Titlel Tayli

2. Repime Eatts Dlinigub

3.Korylonb Derbig

4.Lanterc Karp

"Gather the X-Men! Quickly!"

Test your skills with this X-Men trivia!

1. Who was NOT one of the original X-Men?
    - A. Angel
    - B. Iceman
    - C. Storm
    - D. Beast

2. What is Cyclops's real name?
    - A. Scott Summers
    - B. Bobby Drake
    - C. Peter Parker
    - D. Alex Summers

3. Which of the following powers does Wolverine NOT have?
    - A. Healing factor
    - B. Adamantium claws
    - C. Enhanced senses
    - D. Mind control

4. Where is Professor X's mansion?
    - A. Austin, Texas
    - B. Boston, Massachusetts
    - C. Tampa, Florida
    - D. Westchester, New York

5. Which X-Man is originally from Russia?
    - A. Nightcrawler
    - B. Colossus
    - C. Marvel Girl
    - D. Storm

Can you find the names of the following X-Men in the puzzle below? Look up, down, backwards, forwards and diagonally.

Angel	Iceman
Banshee	Polaris
Beast	Professor X
Colossus	Storm
Cyclops	Wolverine
Havok	

H	S	P	O	L	A	R	I	S	B
C	A	L	P	W	I	C	C	L	A
Y	X	V	W	O	L	V	E	O	N
C	S	T	O	R	M	G	M	R	S
L	P	V	L	K	N	G	A	M	X
O	A	T	S	A	E	B	N	G	E
P	R	O	F	E	S	S	O	R	X
S	E	E	H	S	N	A	B	C	R
C	O	L	O	S	S	U	S	V	M
W	E	N	I	R	E	V	L	O	W

Cyclops, Marvel Girl and Angel arrive in Little Italy.

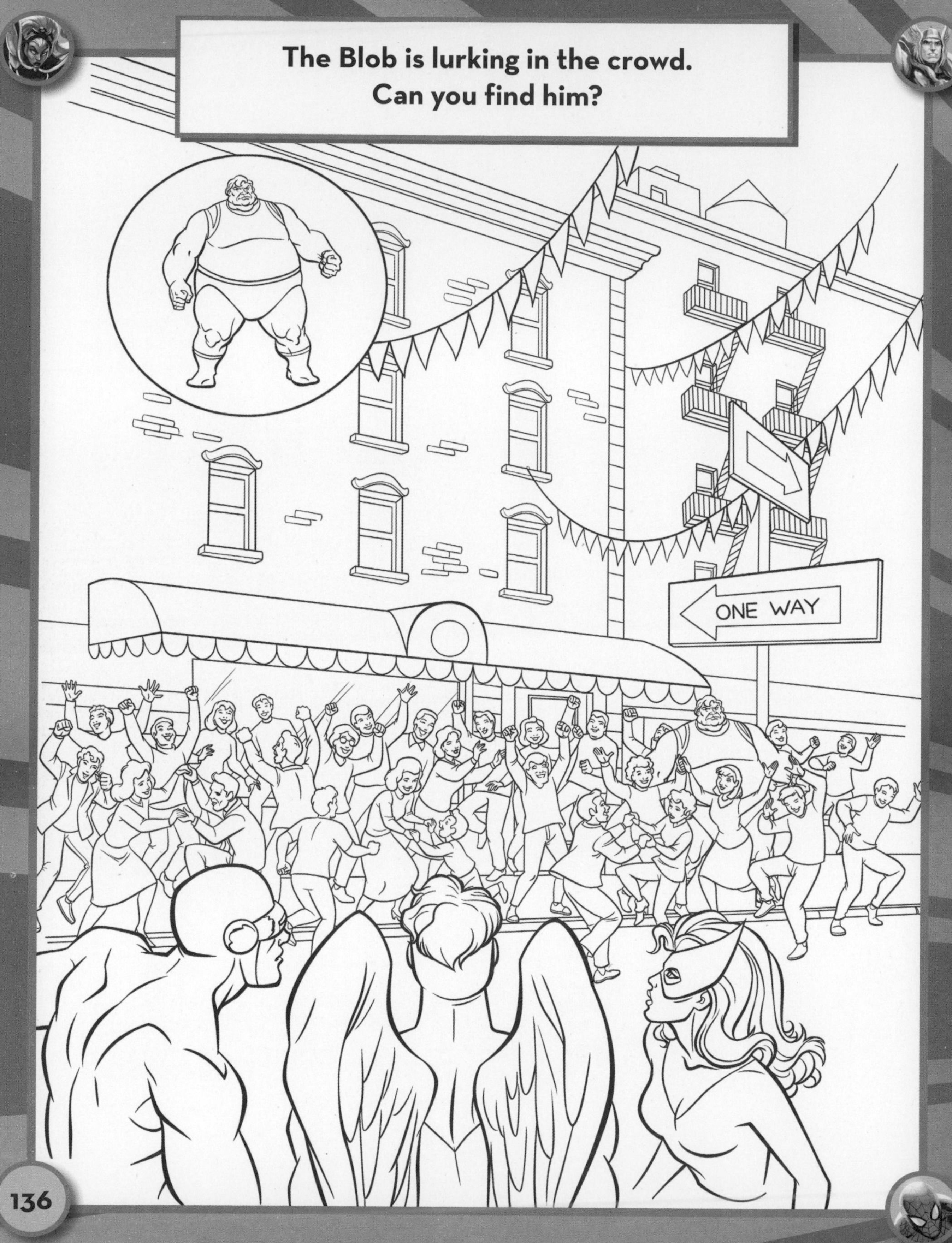
The Blob is lurking in the crowd.
Can you find him?
ONE WAY

The Blob is no pushover.

Help Cyclops choose the right optic blast to take down the Blob.

FINISH

A

B

C

START

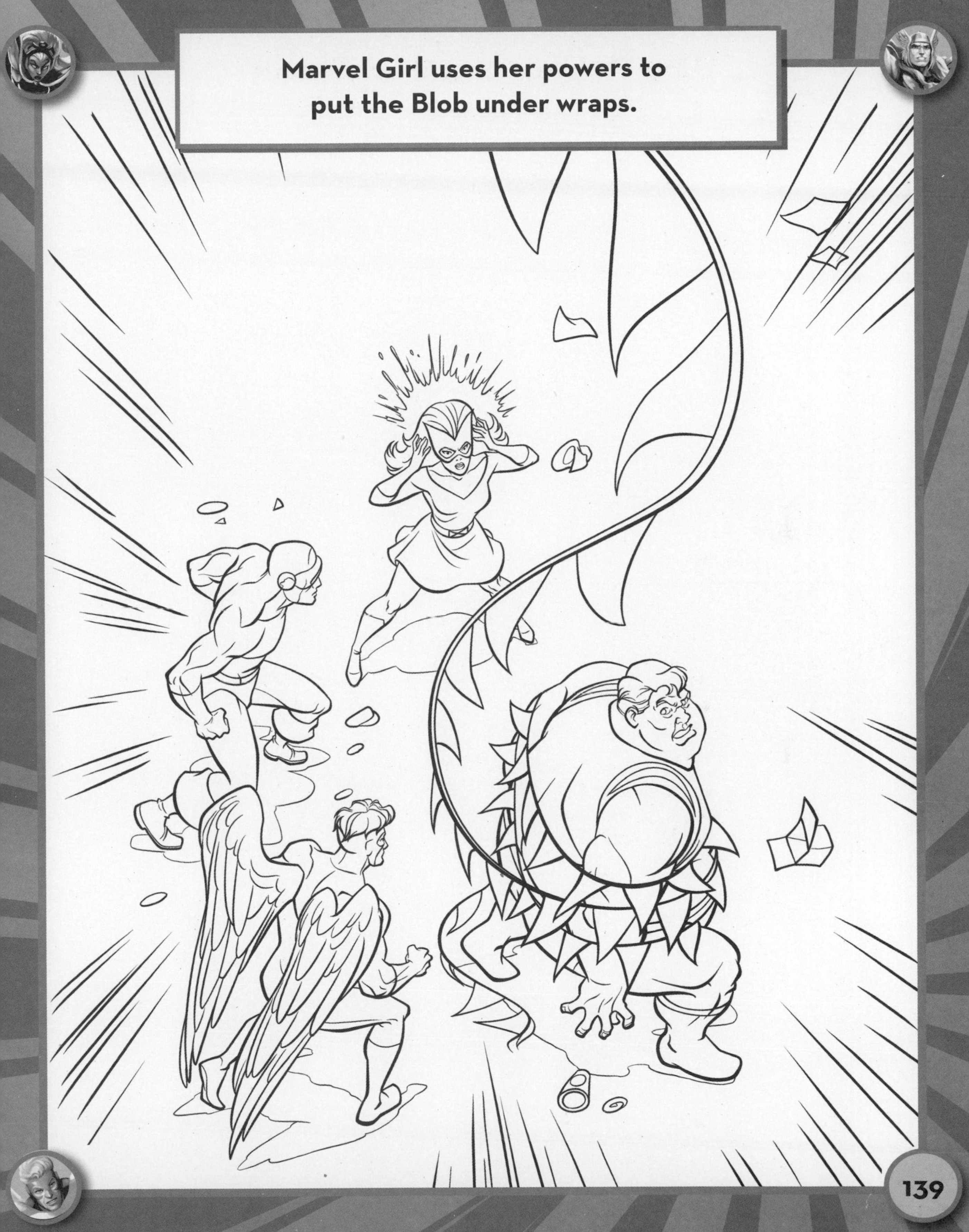
Marvel Girl uses her powers to
put the Blob under wraps.

Which mutant is also Cyclops's brother?

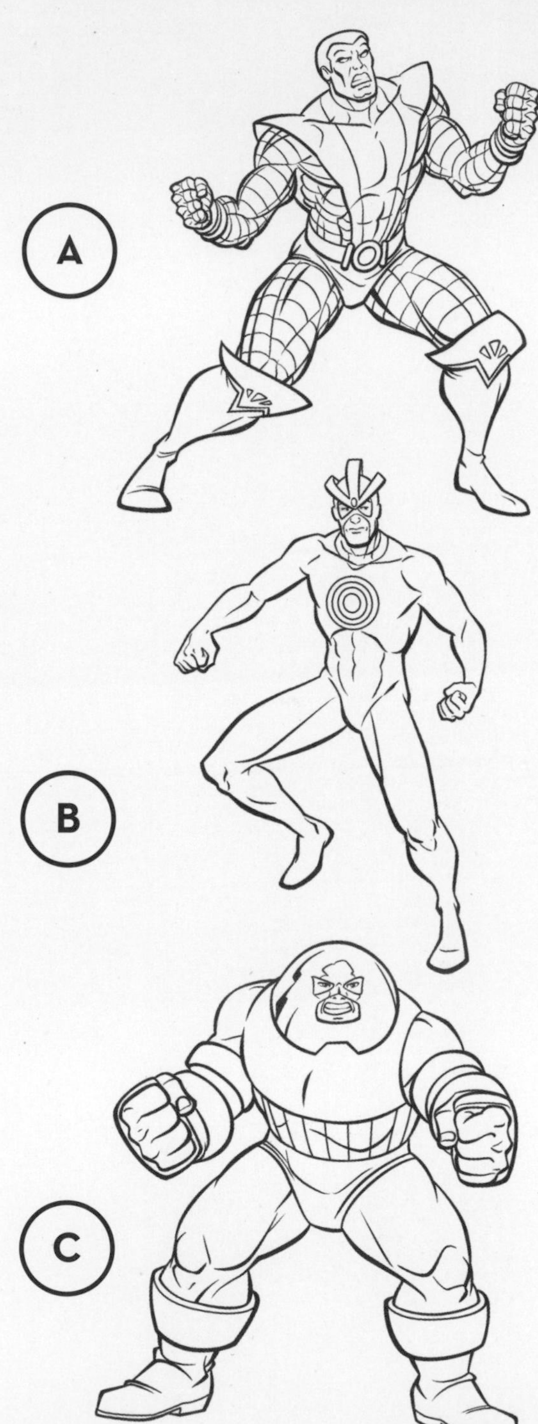

Polaris, Havok and Beast head to the Empire State Building.

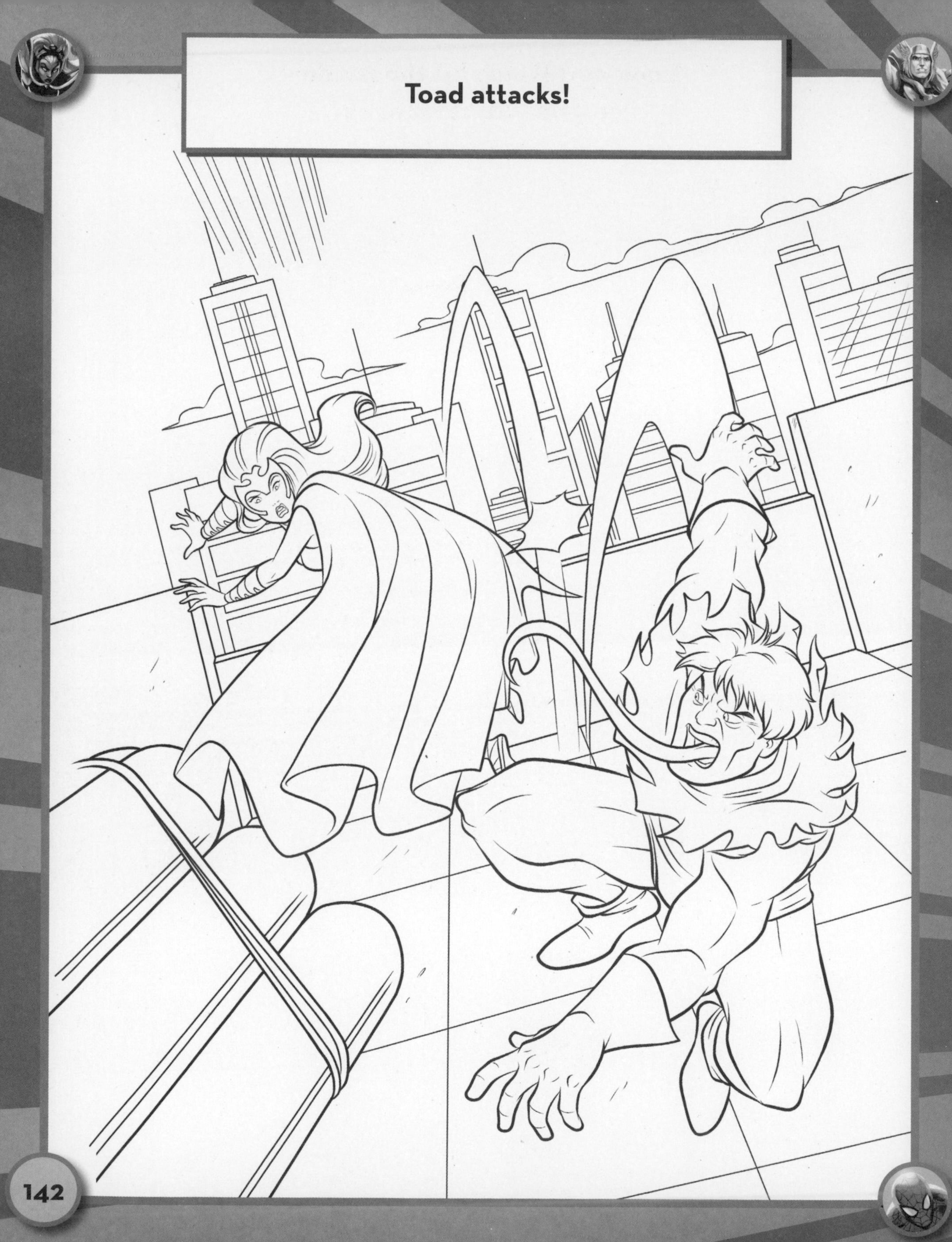

Toad attacks!

Look out! Havok hit the window washer's rig by mistake!

Which rope has the Beast caught? Hopefully it's the right one!

A B C D E

Havok doesn't make the same mistake twice!

Connect the dots to see how Polaris cages Toad.

Iceman, Wolverine and Banshee land at the Brooklyn Bridge.

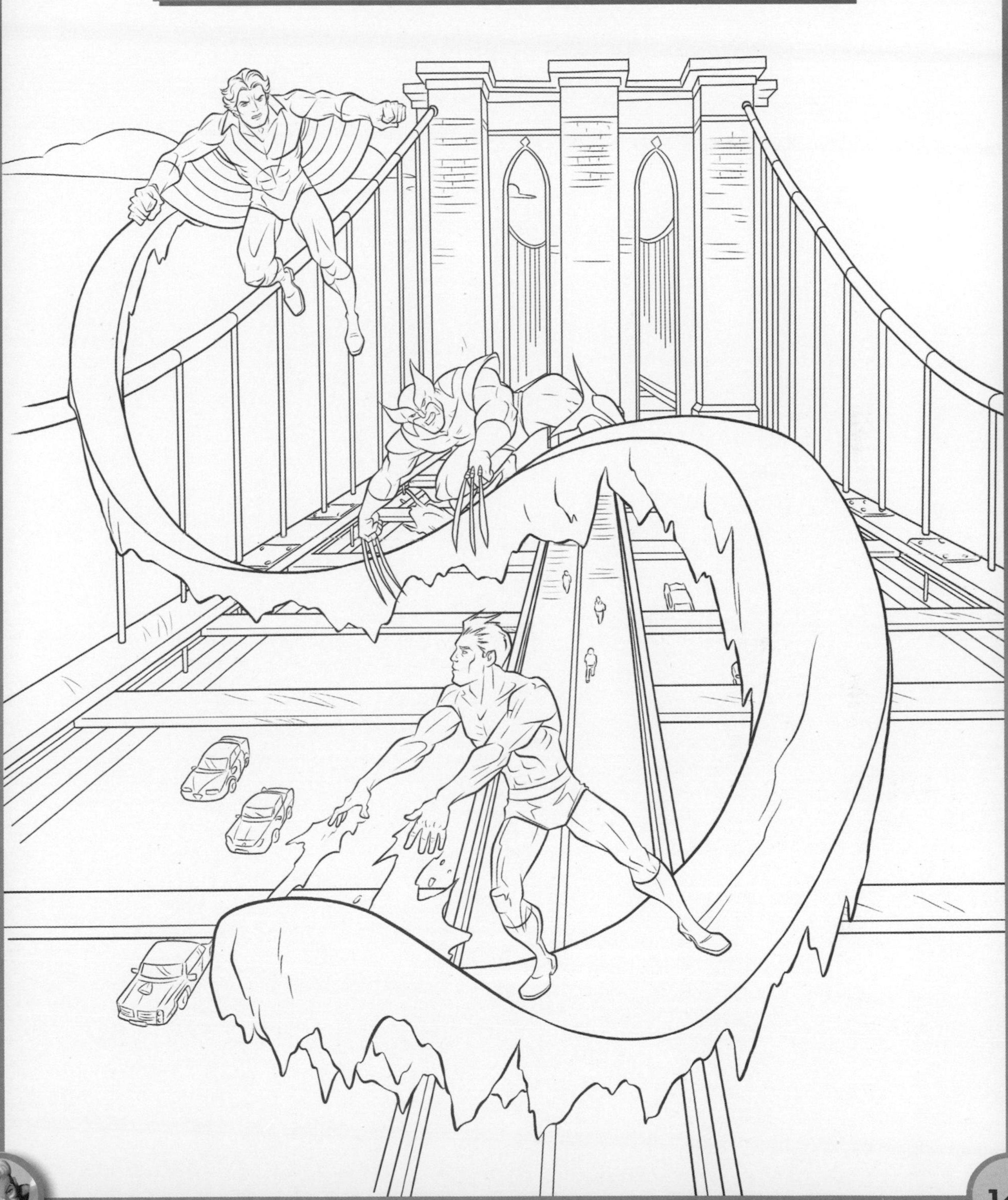

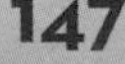

Help Wolverine choose the correct uniform.

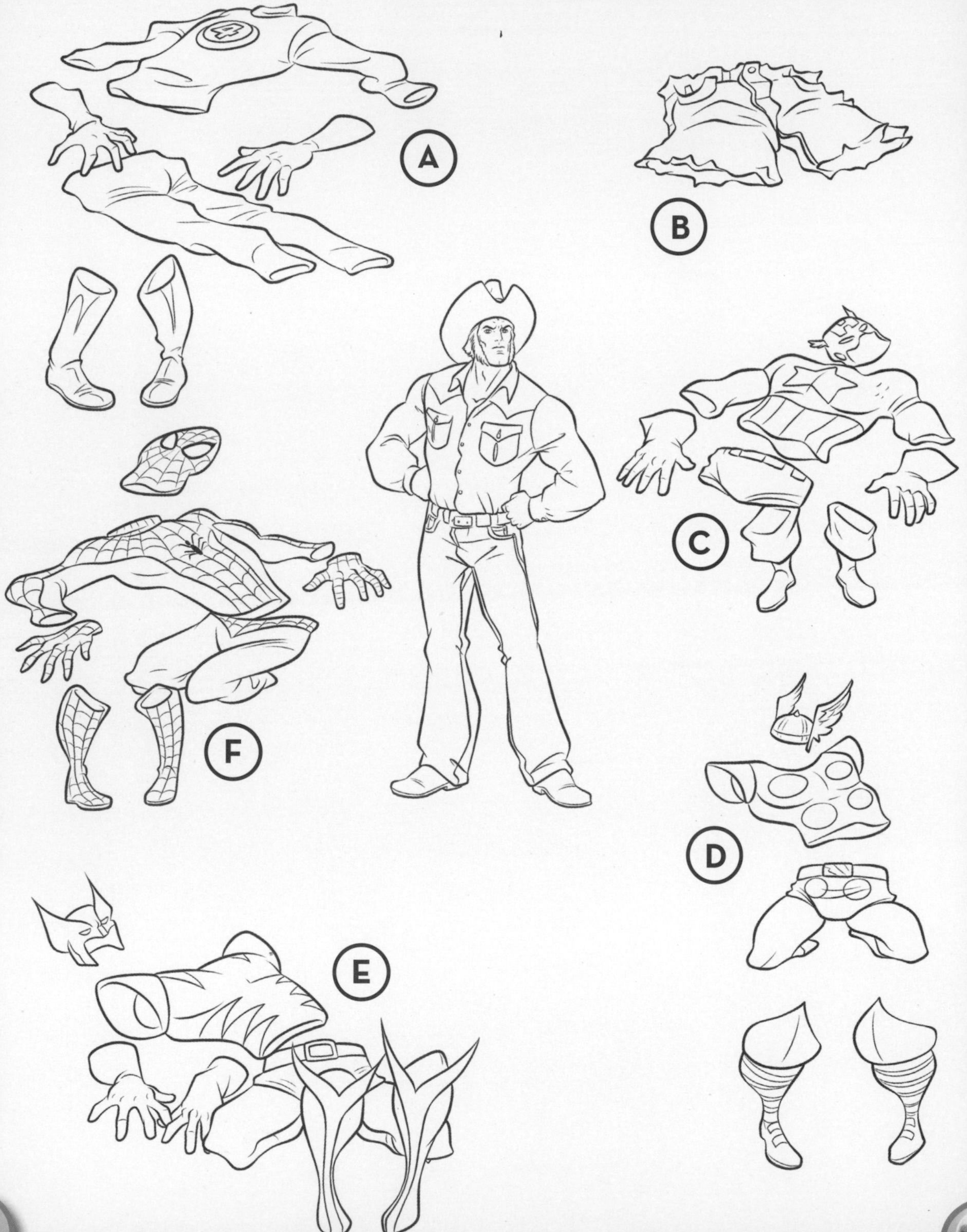

A

B

C

D

E

F

Help the X-Men make their way through the cars to find out what's causing the traffic jam.

FINISH

START

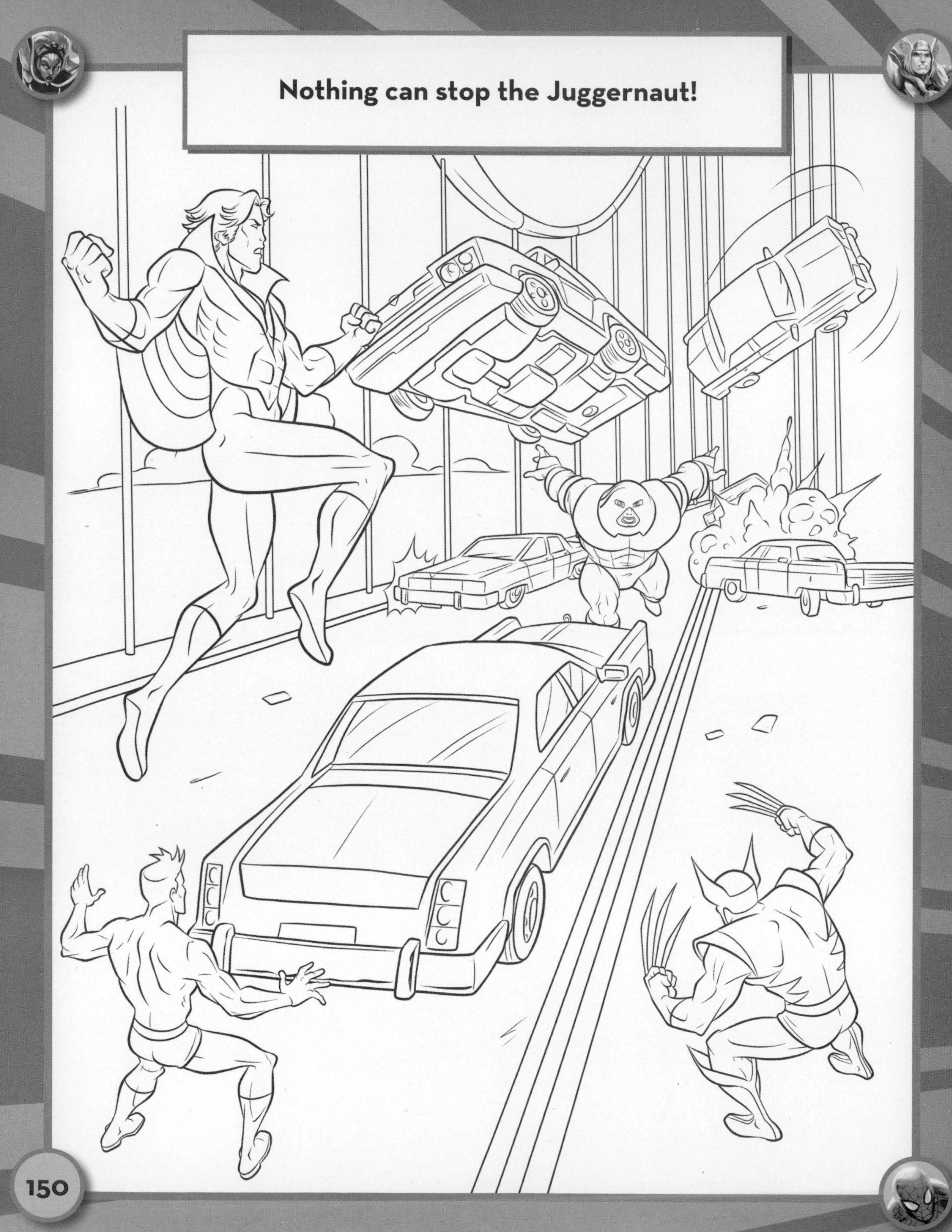
Nothing can stop the Juggernaut!

Banshee unleashes his sonic scream.

Help Iceman catch up to the Juggernaut.

START

FINISH

The bigger they are, the harder they fall.

Time to put the Juggernaut on ice.

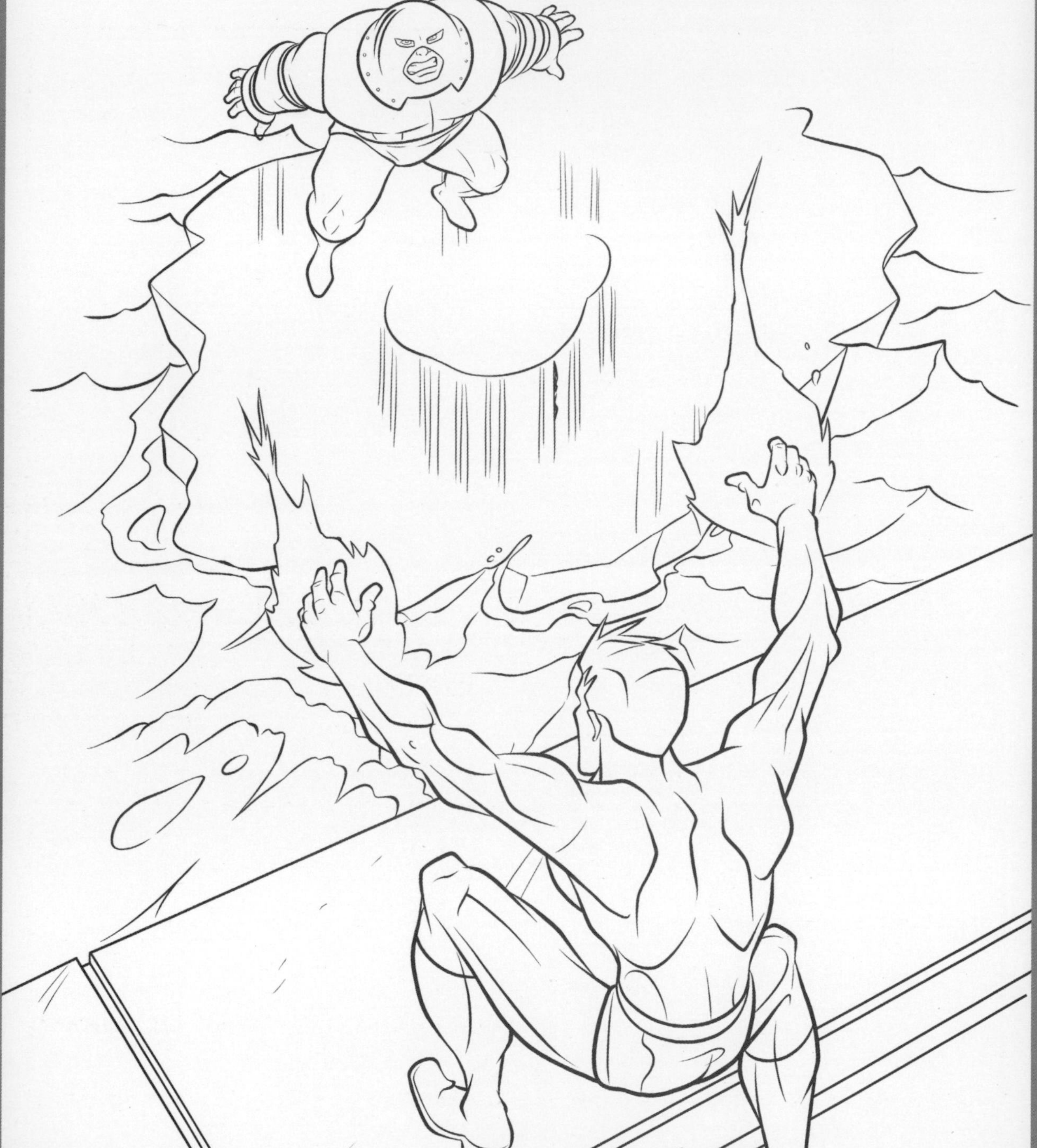

How well do you know the X-Men? Answer the questions and complete the crossword.

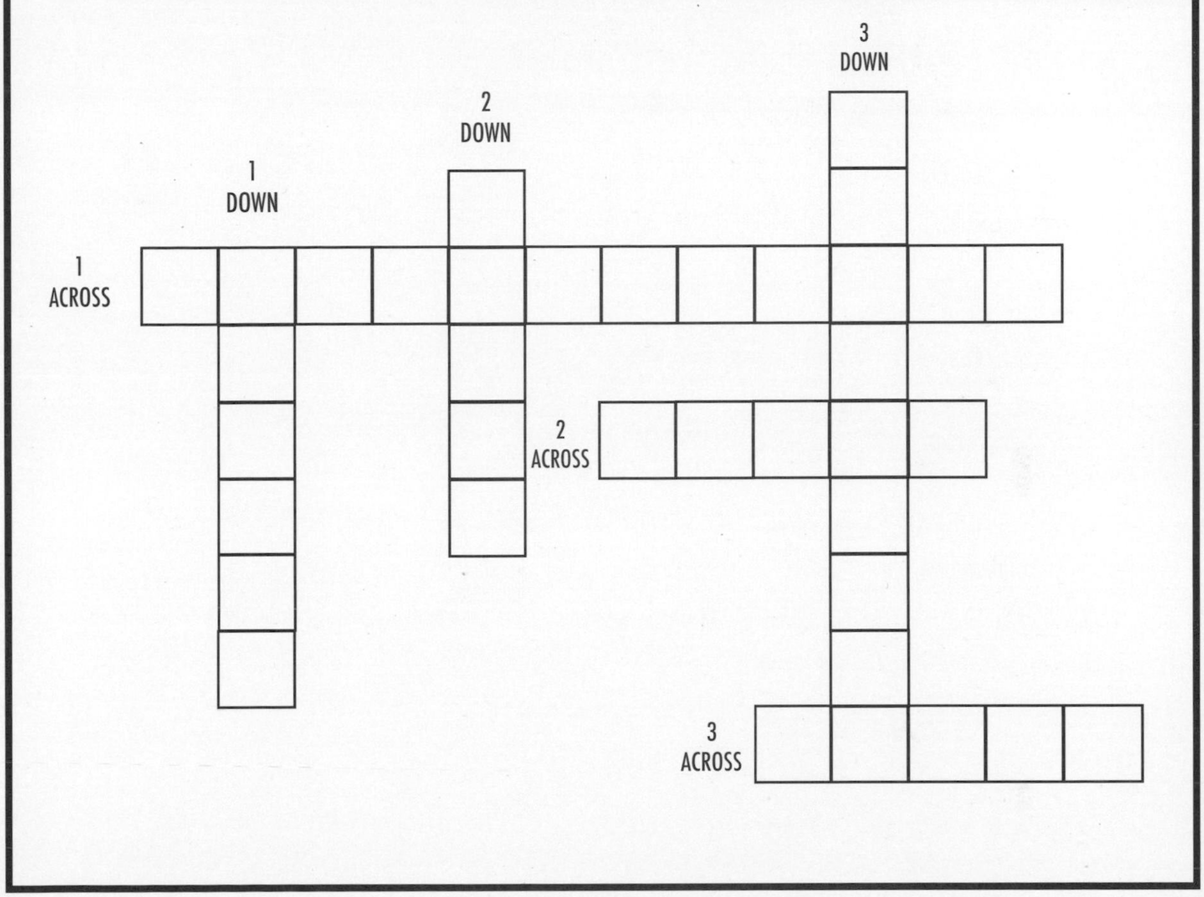

3 DOWN

2 DOWN

1 DOWN

1 ACROSS

2 ACROSS

3 ACROSS

ACROSS

1. Teleporting "Elf"
2. Heavenly Hero
3. Beauty and the ____

DOWN

1. The Coldest X-Man
2. The Weather "Witch"
3. X-Man Known to "Pop" His Claws

Colossus, Storm and Nightcrawler arrive in Central Park.

Can you find five things that are different on this page than on the last page? Circle them.

Who has telekinetic powers like Magneto?

A

B

C

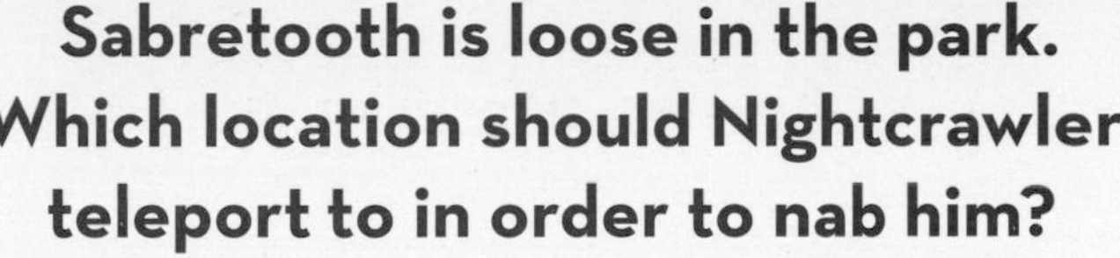

Sabretooth is loose in the park. Which location should Nightcrawler teleport to in order to nab him?

A

B

C

D

E

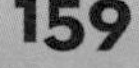

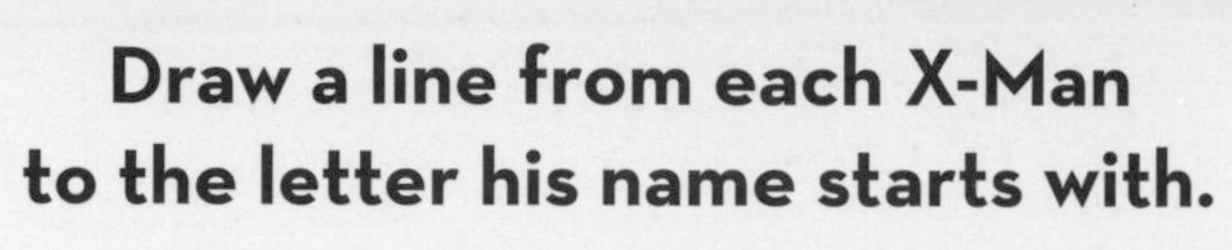

Draw a line from each X-Man to the letter his name starts with.

A

B

C

ANSWER KEY

P49: 1-C, 2-E, 3-D, 4-B, 5-A.

P50:

P53:

P55: Shadow 3.

P56: Symbol A.

P57: Web D.

P58:

P60:

P62: Toy D.

P65:

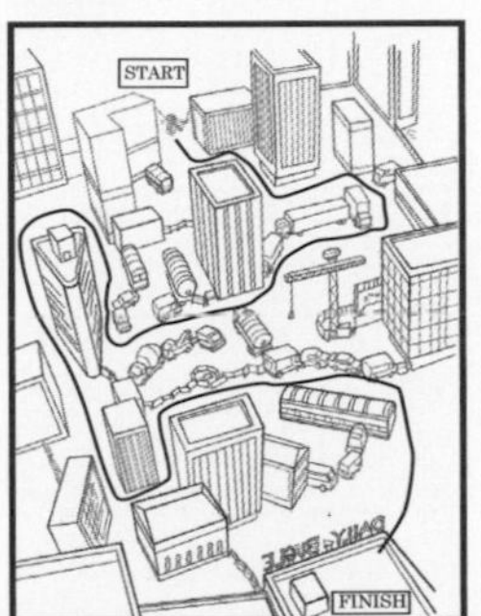

P66: possible answers: bug, hat, lady, legal, glad, late, beagle, lid.

P68: Symbol F.

P69:

P70: ACROSS:1. Peter Parker, 2. Ock, 3. Cat, 4. Water DOWN: 1. Electricity 2. Green 3. Rhino

P72:

P74: Photo B.

P76:

M	Y	S	T	E	R	I	O	Q	C
Y	V	P	B	G	Z	L	E	N	H
E	L	I	Z	A	I	M	A	Y	A
R	Z	D	C	Z	R	O	D	S	M
U	H	E	A	E	M	R	I	E	E
T	Y	R	F	L	O	B	R	M	L
L	D	M	V	M	R	I	O	N	E
U	R	A	A	U	F	U	P	A	O
V	E	N	O	M	L	S	S	Y	N
R	E	T	O	O	H	S	B	E	W

P78: A, D, and E.

P79:

P81: Piece D.

P82: 7 times.

P83: Lift F.

P84: 12 pictures

P85: Web C.

P87: F

P89: ZEMO IS ATTACKING

P96: MJOLNIR

P99:

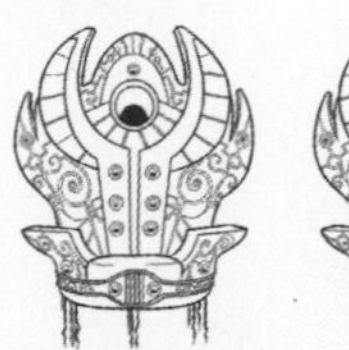

P100: TROLL ATTACK!

P104:

P105:

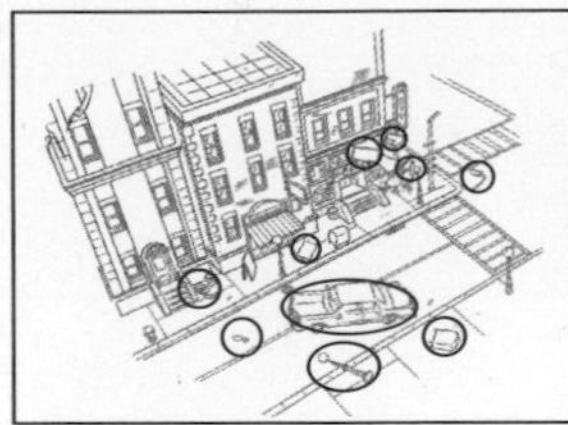

P109:

ANSWER KEY

P110:

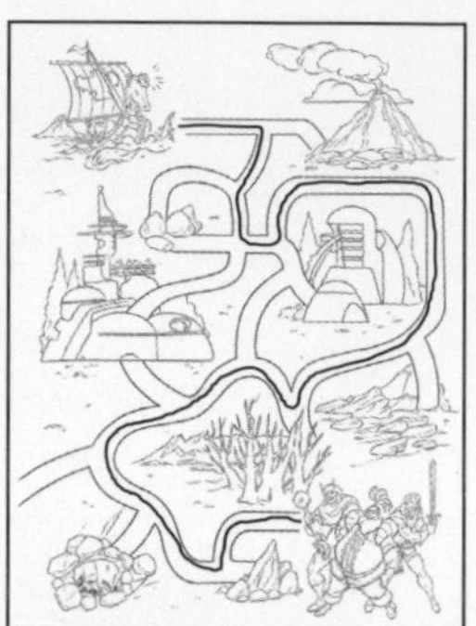

P111: A-2, B-4, C-3, D-1.

P116: FOOL! THOR COMMANDS THE LIGHTNING!

P121: HE HATES WATER!

P127: C.

P130:

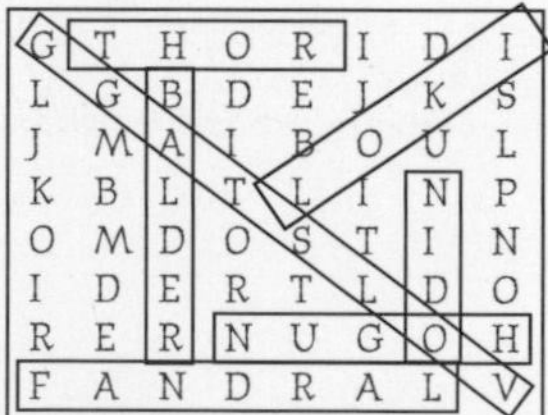

P131: 1. Little Italy, 2. Empire State Building, 3. Brooklyn Bridge, 4. Central Park.

P133: 1. C, 2. A, 3. D, 4. D, 5. B

P134:

P136:

P138: Optic blast B.

P140: B.

P144: Rope D.

P148: Costume E.

P149:

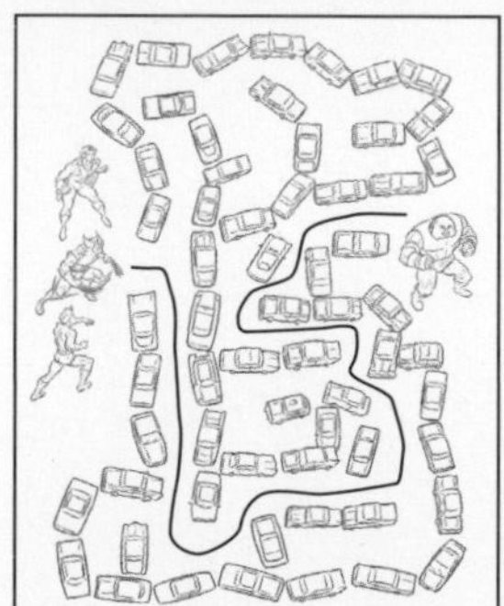

P152:

P155: ACROSS: 1. Nightcrawler, 2.Angel, 3. Beast. DOWN: 1.Iceman, 2.Storm, 3.Wolverine.

P157:

P158: A

P159: Choice E.

P160: A. to Angel, B. to Beast, and C. to Cyclops.

MARVEL

THE MIGHTY THOR™

AN ORIGIN STORY

What would it be like to live among legends?

To be something more than human?

To hold great power in your hands ...

and know how to use it?

To be
feared?

To be

brave,

to be honoured,

to be MIGHTY?

Some are born with these qualities.

And some spend their lives working to attain them.

This is a story about someone who was born into royalty, but needed to earn his honour.

This is a story about a hero …

named THOR.

Thor's realm was called Asgard. It sat like an island where the shores were swept by the sea of space.

The people who lived on Asgard were called Asgardians and the Asgardians called our world Midgard. The only way to reach our world from theirs was by the rainbow bridge, Bifrost. The bridge was guarded by the sentry called Heimdall.

Even though Asgard was well protected, threats were endless.

Thor was one of the land's great protectors.

He was also a prince. He lived with his brother Loki in the castle of their father, Odin.

Thor was arrogant and chose his friends for their loyalty: the brave warrior Balder and a band of soldiers called the Warriors Three – Fandral, Volstagg and Hogun – and the beautiful, strong and wise Lady Sif.

Thor's father, Odin, ruled over all of Asgard.

He and his wife, Frigga, wanted nothing more than for their sons to grow up to be worthy rulers.

But there could only be one supreme ruler of Asgard. Only one who could be like Odin. And even though Loki was thoughtful, clever and quick ...

Thor was firstborn and so the throne was his by right.

To determine when Thor would be ready to rule, Odin had a special hammer made. It was forged from a mystical metal called Uru, which came from the heart of a dying star.

The hammer was named ... Mjolnir and it held great power.

But no one would be able to lift the hammer unless he or she was worthy.

The hammer was immovable to Thor.

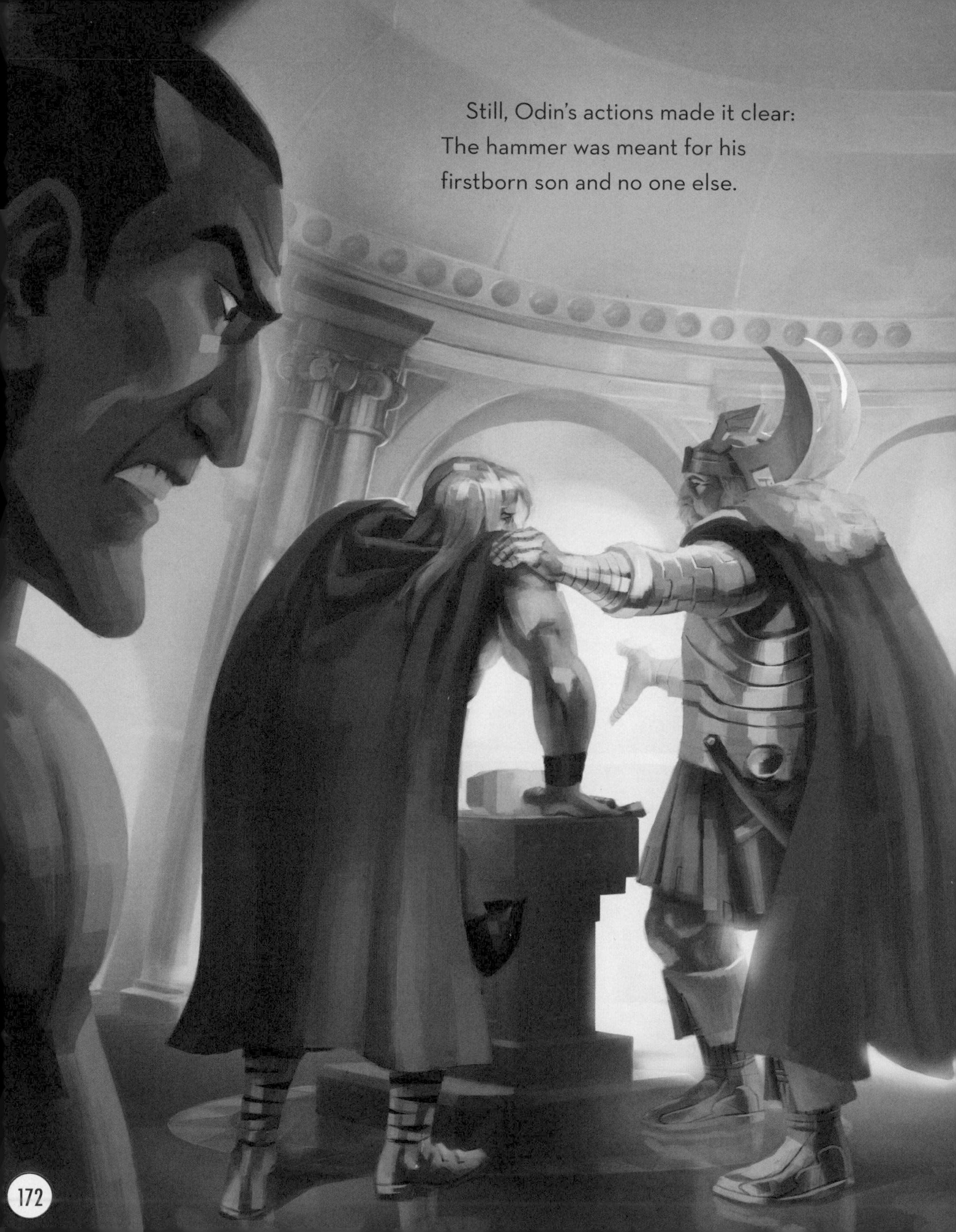

Still, Odin's actions made it clear: The hammer was meant for his firstborn son and no one else.

Even so, proving worthy of Mjolnir was not an easy task.

Thor spent nearly every moment trying to earn his right to hold the hammer. He performed amazing acts of bravery.

He was honoured for acts of nobility.

He demonstrated feats of great strength.

With every great achievement, Thor attempted once more to pick up Mjolnir. It seemed as if he would never raise the hammer more than a few inches from the table.

And then

one day ...

he DID.

Thor had proven himself worthy of his weapon and he used it well. When he threw the hammer, it always returned to him.

When he twirled it by its handle, he could soar like a winged beast!

And when he slammed it twice upon the ground ...

... he could summon all the power of lightning, rain and thunder!

In fact, with his hammer in hand, there was little Thor could not do.

And he knew it.

Odin wanted him to be a great warrior and he had become one. His father wanted him to earn the respect of Asgard. He had it. But then Thor began to let the power go to his head.

And Odin was not happy.

In fact, he had grown quite angry with his son.

Odin called Thor to his throne room. Thor knew that something was wrong. His father rarely summoned him in such a harsh tone. Thor was sure that his jealous brother Loki had spun some lie to get him into trouble.

But nothing could have been further from Thor's mind than what Odin had to say to him.

Odin told Thor that he was his favoured son.

He told him that he was brave beyond compare and noble as a prince must be.

He told him that his strength was legendary and that he was the best warrior in the kingdom.

But Thor did not know what it meant to be weak or to feel pain. And without knowing humility, Thor could never be a truly honourable warrior.

Odin was angry. In his rage, he tore Mjolnir from Thor's hand and threw it towards Midgard. Then he stripped Thor of his armour and sent him to Earth.

Odin made his son believe that he was a medical student with an injured leg, named Don Blake.

As Blake, Thor learned to study hard. At times he thought he might fail. But he worked harder than he ever had in Asgard and in the end he earned his degree.

He allowed others to help him with his injury. In doing so, he discovered that people were generally good. Thor learned to truly love humanity. As a surgeon, he treated the sick.

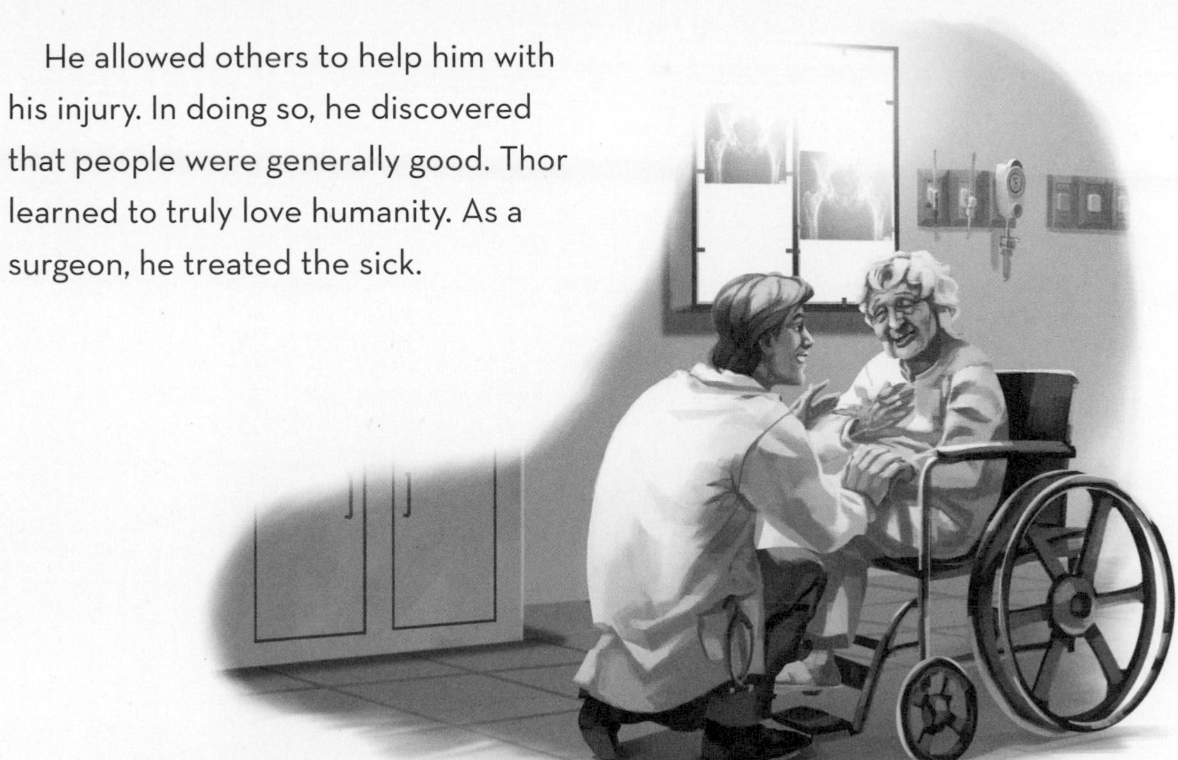

He helped weak people find their strengths.

And one day, while on holiday in Norway ...

Don Blake found himself trapped in a cave. The only possible exit lay behind a boulder.

He found a staff on the ground and shoved it under the boulder. He tried with all his might to move the rock. He pushed and pushed.

He was so angry that he took the staff and struck it on the ground. And that's when it became clear that it was no ordinary stick.

It was Mjolnir in disguise!

Odin had sent Don to this cave. Odin, the All Father of Asgard, was pleased.

His son had learned humility.

He had at long last become a complete hero.

He had become human in spirit, but still, now and forever ...

he was

THE MIGHTY THOR.

MARVEL
THE UNCANNY
X-MEN™
AN ORIGIN STORY

Did you ever have a dream that felt so real, that you were sure you weren't dreaming at all?

This is a story about a boy named Charles Xavier who dreamed he could do many things that an ordinary boy could not.

He dreamed his mind could leave his body and float like a feather.

He dreamed he could know what other people were thinking before they even opened their mouths to speak.

Charles didn't look like other kids, either.

He began to lose his hair at a very young age. And by the time he was a teenager, Charles' head was completely bare.

But that was not all.

Charles had always heard whispers of things that no one was saying out loud. As he grew older, he began to hear them more and more clearly. Eventually Charles realized that he could read minds.

As time went by and Charles grew older, he used his gift to gain knowledge.

He studied to become a doctor of science. He wanted to learn more about why he had these special powers.

Charles soon discovered that he was a mutant – a person born with special abilities.

His studies took him all over the world. And while in Egypt, Charles met another mutant for the first time.

This mutant was evil and Charles had to stop him. So they fought on the astral plane. And Charles won.

Charles soon met another mutant – a man named Erik Magnus.

Magnus had the mutant power to move metal objects without touching them. Charles and Magnus became fast friends. But they did not always agree.

Magnus knew humans feared and hated mutants. He thought the only way for mutants to keep themselves safe was to use their powers to take over the world.

But Charles still dreamed of a world where humans and mutants could live together peacefully.

Charles and Magnus met and defeated an evil human named Baron von Strucker who wanted to use his wealth to destroy anyone he didn't like.

Magnus felt that this proved humans were bad. He took the baron's gold and flew away with it, telling Charles he was foolish to believe that mankind was good.

Charles was sad to lose his friend. As he continued his travels, he began to think about returning home.

But during a stop on his journey, Charles encountered an alien named Lucifer. He wanted to destroy both humans and mutants.

They fought and the alien brought down his secret hideaway on top of Charles. Charles survived, but his legs had been crushed. He would never again be able to walk.

He returned home, more determined than ever to find other mutants. He would train them to fight any threat – mutant, human or alien.

The first mutant Charles found was named Scott Summers. Charles called him Cyclops for the optic blasts he could shoot from his eyes.

Next, Charles and Cyclops rescued a teenager from an angry mutant-hating mob. The boy, Bobby Drake, could turn himself into ice and called himself Iceman.

Then the growing group found Warren Warthington III, who called himself Angel for the wings that helped him fly.

And finally Hank McCoy joined the team. Hank was called The Beast because of his large hands and feet, which helped him swing like a monkey and punch like a gorilla.

Charles renamed the mansion Xavier's School for Gifted Youngsters. To the outside world, it was just another boarding school. But secretly, it was a school for young mutants to learn how to use their powers.

The students were given uniforms and each pledged to fight for Charles' dream.

Charles called himself Professor X and his team the X-Men, because each member had an extraordinary power.

The X-Men soon welcomed their fifth and final founding member – Jean Grey, called Marvel Girl. Jean could move things with her mind.

Professor X then built a computer to locate other mutants. The machine, called Cerebro, showed that a mutant was attacking an army base.

It was the Professor's old friend Magnus!

Now known as Magneto, he had used the baron's gold to wage war on the human race.

Charles knew that only the X-Men could stop his old friend!

The X-Men arrived at the base just as Magneto began to attack.

And so the X-Men sprang into action and attacked him right back.

Cyclops tried to blast through Magneto's magnetic field. But he couldn't.

Magneto guided every missile that Marvel Girl tried to send at him right back at her.

Angel and The Beast did not fare much better.

At last, Magneto attacked them all. But Marvel Girl covered her teammates with a force field.

The X-Men were not so easily defeated!

The X-Men had come to stop Magneto and turn him over to the police. But Magneto had escaped.

The X-Men were disappointed. But Professor X told them he was very proud of them for stopping the attack.

Over the next few months, the X-Men trained in a special gym called the Danger Room. The room was filled with obstacles to help the X-Men perfect their abilities.

And Professor X used Cerebro to keep a constant watch for new mutants.

And he found many! But more often than not, the mutants were evil.

After many battles, the X-Men graduated and became fully-fledged heroes. Professor X had never been prouder of his students.

He retired their school uniforms and dressed them in new costumes. But the end of their school days did not mean the end of their missions. In fact, things only got more difficult for the X-Men.

As mutants grew in number, so did the X-Men. Cyclops' brother Alex Summers – an energy-blasting mutant called Havok – and Lorna Dane, called Polaris for her magnetic abilities, joined the team.

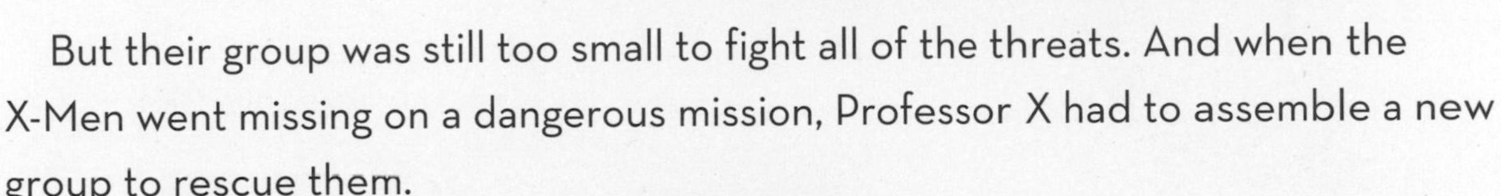

But their group was still too small to fight all of the threats. And when the X-Men went missing on a dangerous mission, Professor X had to assemble a new group to rescue them.

In Canada, he recruited a mutant named Wolverine who could heal himself of any injury and whose claws could cut through almost anything!

In Germany, Charles found Kurt Wagner, called Nightcrawler, who could move from place to place with just a thought.

Together with Wolverine and Nightcrawler, Professor X decided to seek out more good mutants to help rescue the original X-Men.

In Ireland, Charles found Sean Cassidy – Banshee – whose sonic scream could shatter stone and steel.

In Africa, Charles met Ororo Munroe, a weather mutant called Storm.

And in Russia, the mutant Peter Rasputin – called Colossus because he could turn himself to metal – bid a tearful farewell to his family to join the professor.

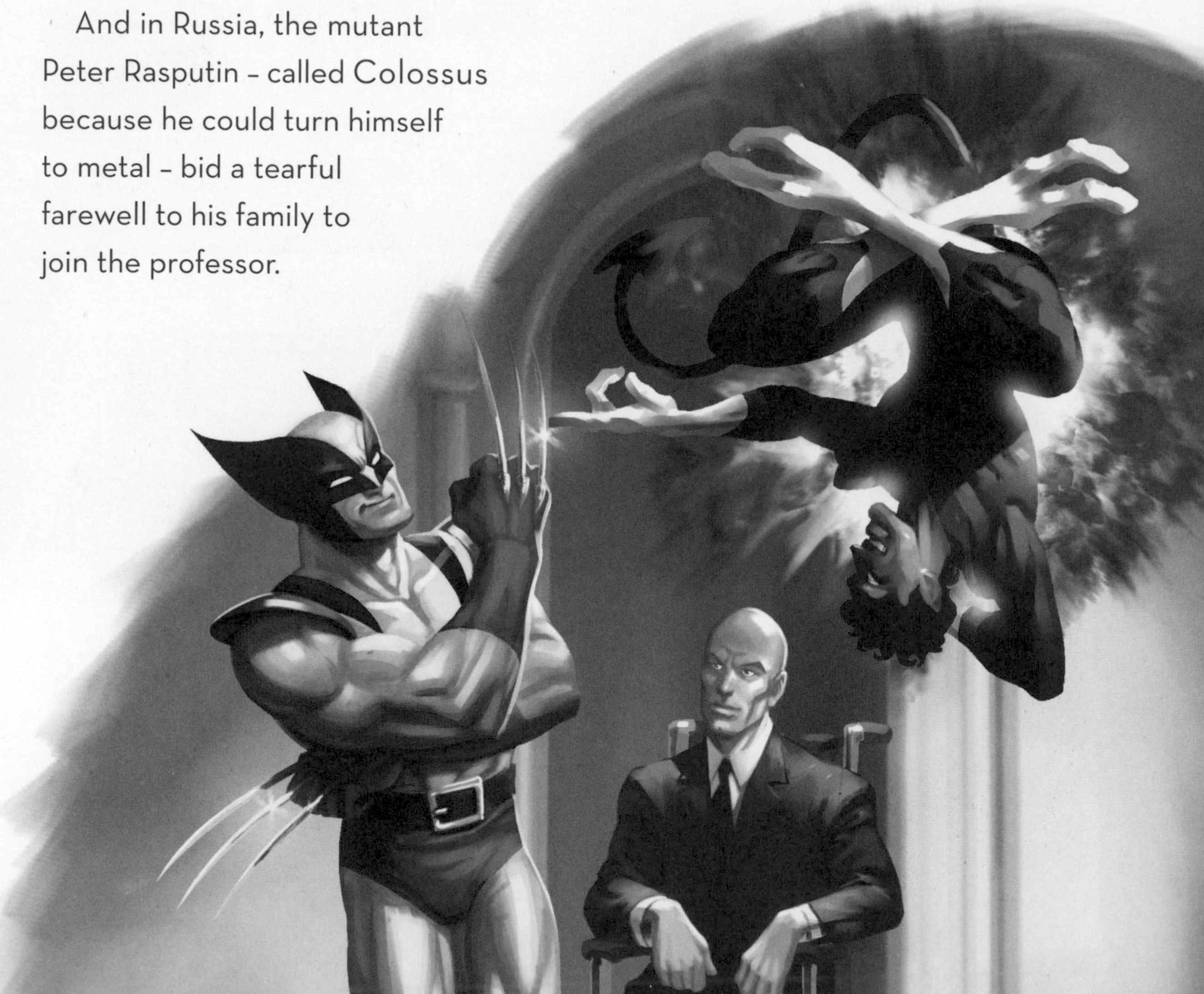

Charles' new international team wasted no time in their search to find the Original X-Men.

The new X-Men rescued the original team from Krakoa, the living island!

The new group decided to stay at Xavier's school.

They trained to use their powers. Soon they too became X-Men.

Although the X-Men were never safe … they were a family.

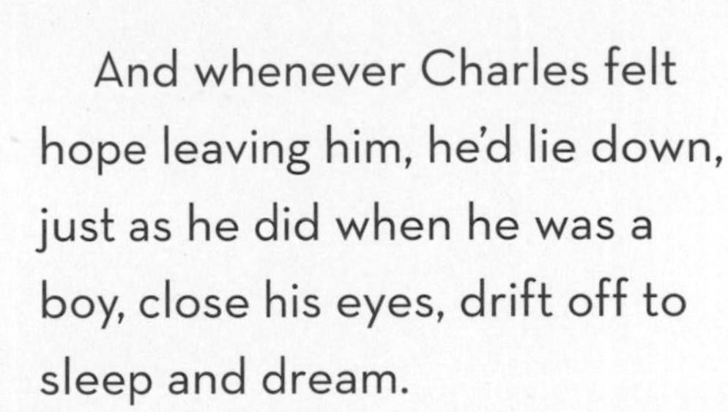

And whenever Charles felt hope leaving him, he'd lie down, just as he did when he was a boy, close his eyes, drift off to sleep and dream.

The X-Men unite!